All the Evidence
You Will Ever Need

All the Evidence
You Will Ever Need

A Scientist Believes in the Gospel of Jesus Christ

PAUL D. BABA

RESOURCE *Publications* · Eugene, Oregon

ALL THE EVIDENCE YOU WILL EVER NEED
A Scientist Believes in the Gospel of Jesus Christ

Wipf & Stock
A Division of Wipf and Stock Publishers
199 W. 8th Ave., Suite 3
Eugene, OR 97401
www.wipfandstock.com

ISBN 13: 978-1-55635-689-6

Manufactured in the U.S.A.

My wonderful wife, June,

Lisa and Karl Lauffer,

Lori and Brent Hagen, Alayna Lauffer,

Christopher Hagen, Curtis Hagen,

Daniel Hagen, Kaylee Hagen,

Matthew Hagen, Michael Hagen,

Mitchell Lauffer

Contents

Preface

With God all things are possible.

Luke 1:39

BACKGROUND

THAT I SHOULD SIT down and write a book is an enigma. Until recently, I had no thoughts of writing a book. As a Ph.D. in a scientific field, a research director, and a division manager, I have been a technical writer for many years. Most programs required lengthy proposals or justifications to obtain funding from government, commercial, or internal sources. Once a program was launched, each one required monthly or quarterly progress reports, and at the conclusion of a phase of the work, a final report. Frequently, I made presentations at scientific symposiums. Some of these expositions were invited talks requested by the particular professional society sponsoring the symposium. The research and development efforts reported on in the presentations were usually published soon after in the appropriate technical journals. In addition, numerous patent applications resulted from the development activities, and these applications required a considerable amount of writing before a patent was issued.

I say all of this to indicate that technical and business writing was endemic to my career for many years. However, it was not the favorite part of my work. I loved doing experiments and directing the studies of the groups within my laboratories. The writing was a necessity to be able to do the programs. Beyond that, I rarely thought about other forms of writing. At times, as an occasional reader of fiction, I have on rare occasions thought about writing a novel. I particularly enjoy reading mysteries. However, it never progressed beyond the infrequent fantasy stage. So, how did I come to write a book?

A couple of years ago, I was thinking about my belief system, and I decided to write down a list of reasons why I believe in the Gospel of Jesus Christ. There was no particular motive other than I felt there were many reasons, based on evidence. I wanted to see how many I could come up with. A recent update to that list became the basis for this book. At the time, I had no idea I would have enough material for a book. Because I felt others would benefit from these ideas, I decided to write up the ideas and see where they could be used. Perhaps, they would be useful in high school, college, or adult Sunday school classes. The material could be useful in church youth programs.

As I started to compose this work, a strange thing occurred. I was enjoying it, and I really felt compelled to write down my thoughts. Moreover, ideas started to flood my mind. I had to have a pen and paper with me all the time, as the ideas came from many sources. Our church offers excellent adult Sunday school classes with very comprehensive teaching. As I sat in these classes, the teaching or class discussion would kick off a whole bunch of ideas for the book almost every week.

Hearing sermons in church frequently led to ideas which I feverishly wrote down. I heard references to scripture verses from such sermons and realized they also had application to my pursuit. My reading also led to ideas. However, most amazing of all, is how I would be driving our car or my truck, and thoughts just came into my mind. At first, I would scramble for pen and paper as I sped down the freeway. Then I started to take a microrecorder with me to record such ideas so I would not crack up my vehicle trying to drive and write at the same time!

Ideas emerged all the time. Moreover, they were ideas that fit into my basic list of reasons. I even kept the microrecorder by my bedside. In the middle of the night, thoughts would arise that I entered into the microrecorder so I could go back to sleep. The outpouring of these ideas made me appreciate how the Holy Spirit may have inspired Biblical writers to generate their material. While this tome does not compare to the Bible, I really feel that my thoughts have come from the Holy Spirit. I do not believe this work came about because I thought it would be nice to write a book. Nor was I interested in enhancing my reputation or making money. I believe the Holy Spirit led me to make my list and inspired me to go beyond merely compiling a list for no reason.

MY JOURNEY IN BRIEF

I have been a Christian for over 60 years. During those years, there has been a progression of spiritual growth that was very unsteady in my early years. During those early years, at times, there were doubts. There were college professors who presented biased information clearly intended to undercut faith. Some of this information was based on the professors' selective interpretations of the Bible. In a geology class during my sophomore year in college, the professor devoted his last lecture of the course to items intended to undermine faith. He allowed no questions, opinions, or discussion in that last class. How about that for enlightened academic discourse!

As the years progressed, I learned there were excellent answers to such misinformation. My spiritual journey was aided by many sources, such as excellent sermons by a long line of brilliant pastors. There were my studies of a wealth of Christian literature covering areas of theology, apologetics, the relationship of science and Christianity, etc. There were Bible-study groups where we wrestled with the meaning of scriptural passages. Out of these interactions, a faith emerged that grew stronger and stronger over the years.

I do not want to give the impression the road was smooth or that the growth was steady. There were many ups and downs. There were extremely difficult events that tested my faith. Christians are not promised a "bed of roses." However, faith in the Lord is an incredible help in times of crisis. I do not know how nonbelievers get through the difficult times of life without faith in the Lord. Because of my experiences, some of which are the subject of a later chapter, I decided to set down information I hope will be helpful to anyone who is interested in strengthening their faith.

I also must add that this effort benefited me immensely. There is the old adage, "the teacher learns more than the students." I trust that is not the case here, for I sincerely hope whoever reads this book will read many of the recommended books cited at the end of many of the chapters and become an expert in matters that strengthen faith. However, researching this book was great fun, and I was able to add considerably to my understanding of the subjects covered here. I hope even mature readers of this work will enjoy similar benefits.

THE PURPOSE

The purpose of this book is to provide evidence for five categories of individuals who have an interest in spiritual matters:

1. For seekers who want to understand the logic of Christianity;

2. For new Christians who may have accepted the Lord in "blind faith;"

3. For mature Christians who may have never gone into their belief system in depth;

4. For Christians with unbelieving friends and family; and

5. For parents of students who are bludgeoned with erroneous teaching that may turn them away from their Christian beliefs.

The material that follows aims to show there are lots of reasons to believe in the Gospel of Christ, and more explicitly, why I believe in the Gospel of Christ. In the following pages, I present much factual material from the scriptures and other sources, and I augment this information with my personal experiences and the experiences of others.

Why do Christians want to share these concepts? There are those who resent the idea of one expressing his or her faith. Religion is supposed to be a private matter. To discuss one's beliefs borders on a taboo in our culture. Certainly, my purpose is not to *impose* my will on anyone else. The emphasis is on *sharing*. When one finds something of value, he or she enjoys sharing it with friends out of love. For example, suppose I had found out about a new cure for cancer that did not involve the terrible treatments of chemotherapy, radiation, or surgery. Would I not be remiss if I did not share that information with an afflicted person about whom I care?

Second, Jesus gave his followers instructions to "Go into all the world and preach the good news to all creation. Whoever believes and is baptized will be saved, but whoever does not believe will be condemned" (Mark 16:15–16). These are strong words, but they also are words of "tough love." It was his intention that all would be able to hear the words of the Gospel and come into his kingdom. In Mark 13:45–46, Jesus says, "Again, the kingdom of heaven is like a merchant looking for fine pearls. When he found one of great value, he went away and sold everything he had and bought it." Nothing we possess can compare with the value of coming into Jesus' kingdom!

OTHER SOURCES

A few of the early chapters of this book reprise information available elsewhere. There are other books dealing with the subject of Christian apologetics and evidence for Christianity. Some even have the word evidence in the title, and they are worthwhile books to read. I have distilled down the information from these books, my own ideas, and other sources, so the reader does not have to obtain numerous other sources to come up with the same conclusions. I have read many of these sources, and I cite references in footnotes and in recommended reading lists for those who desire to go into more depth. Although I cover topics found in some of these books, such as fulfilled prophecy, the problems with a creator-less evolution, etc., my work has a number of chapters on subjects I have not seen expounded upon elsewhere.

At this point, I wish to explain the citation of Bible verses for those who are not familiar with these notations. The books of the Bible are listed in the front of every Bible. So, if you might have difficulty locating where books are in your Bible, just check the Table of Contents. All the books are listed there with their page numbers. The common notations are as follows: Book Title, followed by the Chapter, followed by a colon, then the verses. For example, a reference above, given as Mark 13:45–46, refers to the book of Mark, chapter 13, and verses from 45 to 46.

DENOMINATIONS

It is also important to understand the concept of denominations. Denominations are groups of churches, synagogues, temples, etc. that have organized into a federation based on commonality of beliefs. Typically, the central tenets of the Bible are not at issue in the establishment of denominations. Rather, there are usually peripheral issues about which persons of belief feel strongly and are the basis for their formation of subsets of the major groups, such as Protestantism, Orthodoxy, etc.

I emphasize that this book is not intended to be denominationally oriented. Persons of the major faiths should find commonality in this book. There are areas of the book that are consistent with Judaism. It is my belief, and the belief of many others, that Christianity is the logical extension of Judaism. After all, every author of the Bible with probably one exception was a Jew. I further hope this book will appeal to people of faiths that are not considered above, and especially those who are not part of any particular belief system.

JARGON

Finally, a word about jargon. In many areas of life, jargon develops that is unique to certain walks of life. Christianity is no different. Many terms have arisen over centuries that are particular to Christianity. I have endeavored to exclude such terms as much as possible. However, where a term is necessary for the context of the discourse, I have tried to explain the term to provide clarity.

Acknowledgments

M ANY PERSONS HAVE MADE contributions to the publication of this book. I extend my gratitude to all of them.

My wife June has been an encourager all through the process. She has read all of the materials and has made many helpful comments.

My daughter Lori, my great friend and author Lee Horsman, and June spent considerable efforts and time in reviewing the entire final manuscript, and each one suggested changes that improved the document.

Early in the process I gave copies of initial chapters to a number of persons for their comments: Rev. Gary Gaddini; my daughter and professional editor, Lisa Lauffer; Prof. Arthur Patzia; Dr. Peter Payne; and Rev. Rod Toews. All contributed many insights that strengthened those early writings. Lisa did extensive editing, suggested a number of style changes, and came up with the title for the book.

Author Dan Kline, Senior Editor David Kopp, Author Cindy Martinusen, and Literary Agent Bucky Rosenbaum all reviewed versions of my proposal at two writers' conferences. The result was an improved proposal.

Rick Schneider and Ken Olson both expended efforts to contact publishers and agents to promote the proposal. It was Ken who led me to Wipf and Stock, the publishers of this book.

Carrie Wolcott, project manager, and Jim Tedrick, managing editor, at Wipf and Stock Publishers, were very helpful at various stages of the production process, making many worthwhile suggestions.

Introduction

You Mean There's Evidence?

The heavens declare the glory of God;
the skies proclaim the work of his hands.

Psalms 19:1

IT'S A BOOK ABOUT EVIDENCE

Is THIS BOOK A proof? No, but this is a book that is largely about evidence. The premise of this book is that if one has the faith to accept Jesus Christ as Savior, there is a large body of evidence lending tremendous support to that faith. However, it is important to ascertain that this work does not purport to be a proof. Faith is still the cornerstone of Christianity. If one could truly prove beyond all doubt that God exists and that he sent his Son, Jesus Christ, to die for our sins, all need for faith is removed. Every reasonable and intelligent person would believe, and we would be effectively reduced to robots. Now this comment may send many readers to the exits. It is the usual disclaimer that is made, albeit true, that leaves the seeker with no other alternatives. Many persons believe that faith in Jesus Christ is "blind faith"; in fact, some might say "blind faith" is a necessity. Actually, faith may start in simplicity; however, God has given us in nature and in the Bible much information that forms a logical foundation for our faith. Please stay tuned. There is a lot more to the story.

THE CONCEPT OF EVIDENCE

Imagine a case in which someone is accused of murder. A person has gone missing. The evidential factors usually apparent in a murder victim's body are not known. No weapon has been found. However, there is a single witness. A neighbor has seen the couple arguing shortly before the spouse has been reported to the police as missing. There are a few other nebulous factors pointing to the missing person's spouse as a suspect.

We have heard of many such cases. The police go to great lengths to recover a body. Exhaustive searches take place, but no body is located. Experienced crime scene investigators examine the home extensively. Very little evidence is turned up. Based on the one witness's testimony, it is suspected the missing person's spouse has committed the crime. However, due to the paucity of evidence, no charges are made. No court would convict on the evidence at hand.

Imagine the same case with many evidential factors. The spouse is found in a shallow grave in a field near the home. The spouse has died from numerous stab wounds. Material under the victim's nails and analysis show that the material contains her husband's (or his wife's) DNA. A knife is found in a dumpster near the house. It is from a distinctive kitchen set, and blood on the knife is shown to belong to the victim. It is learned the suspect's business was in financial difficulty and that he (or she) took out a large insurance policy on the spouse recently. A number of witnesses in the neighborhood attest to numerous heated arguments between the two, and there are police reports of physical abuse. Moreover, a lover is discovered who admits to a plot to get rid of the spouse.

Yes, I know; I have really set this case up, but I know that you get the idea. Although I have brought in many factors, the evidence is still circumstantial. No witness has seen the killing, but the more evidence that piles up, the more solid is the case. The large body of evidence strengthens the case for a guilty verdict. Although any one item may be explained away, the totality of the body of evidence makes a strong case that makes a jury likely to convict.

It is my intention to show there is a large body of evidence for the Gospel of Jesus Christ that is vital to my faith. Our faith is not "blind faith," as many persons assert. God still wants our faith, but I believe he is gracious in providing evidence to build up our faith. Any one of the individual evidential elements I will discuss may be given alternative explanations. However, taken together, they bolster my faith, and the point of this work is to explain why I believe. It is up to the reader to decide for himself or herself whether the case is convincing.

Second, faith in the Gospel of Jesus Christ is not primarily an emotional experience. A decision to accept Christ as Savior often affects the emotions, as one experiences the grace of God; but more importantly, it is a logical intellectual decision. For example, the apostle Paul went to great lengths in the New Testament to show the logic of the Gospel. He often appealed to the intellect, not the emotions. I raise this point at this time, because the essence of this work is that there are logical reasons to believe in the gospel of Christ.

A LOGICAL THOUGHT PROCESS

Step One: Is There an Intelligent Designer?

I propose a three-step logical process that should guide a seeker's thoughts in determining a belief system. The first step is to consider whether or not there is a creator or, as has become popular in many circles, an "intelligent designer." If one sees no reason to believe in an intelligent designer, the process ends in atheism or agnosticism for that person. If a person sees that there is extensive evidence for intelligent design, he or she may be encouraged to consider the second step. Chapter One provides the evidence for an intelligent designer.

Step Two: Did the Creator Leave Us with a Manual?

For those who are convinced that Chapter One provides clear evidence for a creator, what is the next step? Is it really important? Do not all religions lead to God? No, not if one believes that the Bible is God's word. There are significant contradictions between the Bible and all other religions. The Bible and the "manuals" for these other religions cannot stand side by side. But what is the evidence for the Bible's preeminence? In Part Two, I discuss why the Bible is unique and why I believe it is the only "user's manual" from God. By the end of Part Two, I anticipate and hope most readers will agree with this point.

Step Three: What Does the Bible Tell Us About the Way to Eternal Life?

The Bible clearly teaches the way into the Kingdom of God is through the Gospel of Jesus Christ. One needs to understand and accept that he or she is a sinner. Romans 3:23 states this fact unequivocally, "For all have sinned and fall short of the glory of God." But illustrative of God's incredible love, the apostle Peter tells us that God does not want anyone to perish, "He is patient with you, not wanting anyone to perish, but everyone to come to repentance" (2 Peter 3:9).

The most famous verse in the Bible gives us the "Gospel in a nutshell": "For God so loved the world that he gave his one and only Son, that whoever believes in him shall not perish but have eternal life" (John 3:16). So, accepting Christ's incredible sacrifice on the cross and appropriating that sacrifice for the forgiveness of one's sins allows one to be totally forgiven and accepted into God's kingdom.

Part One
Is There a Creator?

1

The Problems with Evolution

But God chose the foolish things of the world to shame the wise.

1 Corinthians 1:27

DO WE "HAVE EVOLUTION"? DO WE NEED GOD?

THE FIRST STEP IN a logical thought process in developing a person's belief system is to deal with the question about whether or not God or an Intelligent Designer exists. Many years ago, there was a brilliant physicist in a research group I managed. We were working on unique magnetic materials for microwave applications, and this man was doing excellent work. We became good friends and often engaged in interesting conversations. I learned a lot about his experiences as a young person growing up in India. One day we were discussing our beliefs about God, and his position was, "We have evolution. Why do we need God?" This position has been stated by many to be the belief systems of all scientists in opposition to the positions of believers in a creator. As will be shown, this conclusion is patently false.

Unfortunately, because of the rise of the *theory* of evolution taught as the *fact* of evolution, many pastors and television evangelists expound on the subject, "science versus religion." True science is not the enemy of religion. True science is all about finding the truth about nature. Truth about nature means going where the facts lead the investigator, not ignoring the facts because the investigator has a belief in a theory. Truth in nature should include the recognition of flaws in theories as well as the clear findings of fact about any theory, positive or negative—yes, that includes the theory of evolution.

A QUIET REVOLUTION: SCIENTISTS AS DEISTS

For decades, there has been a quiet revolution going on in scientific circles, but much more slowly in educational circles. School teachers and school books seem to be way behind the times, still teaching evolution as a fact. In many cases, the quiet revolution is being promulgated not by Christians or pastors or by "dogmatic religionists." Many technical persons have become believers in intelligent design and a creator, but there are those who are not believers in the God of the Bible—yet.

However, there is information that may give some insight into the fact that it is not a given that scientists do not believe in intelligent design. The editors of the book, *Cosmos, Bios, Theos,* provided six questions to sixty eminent scientists.[1] Among the disciplines were astronomy, mathematics, physics, biology, and chemistry. All of the scientists were highly accomplished in their fields, and twenty-four of them were Nobel Prize winners. One of the questions dealt with their belief in God or a creator. Forty of them, or two thirds, believed in some kind of intelligent designer or creator.

The late Professor Arthur Schawlow, who was a friend of mine at Bell Telephone Laboratories, was a Nobel Prize winner and a devout Christian. His brother-in-law, Professor Charles Townes, also a Nobel Prize winner for his work leading to the invention of the laser, is also a Christian. Professor Christian Anfinsen, who did not indicate the extent of his religious beliefs, said, "I think only an idiot can be an atheist. We must admit that there exists an incomprehensible power or force with limitless foresight and knowledge that started the whole universe going in the first place."[2]

AMERICAN SCIENTIFIC AFFILIATION

The American Scientific Affiliation (ASA) "is a fellowship of men and women of science and disciplines that can relate to science, who share a common fidelity to the Word of God and a commitment to integrity in the practice of science. The stated purpose of the ASA is to investigate any area relating Christian faith and science and to make known the results of such investigations for comment and criticism by the Christian com-

1. Prof. Henry Margenau and Roy Varghese, editors, *Cosmos, Bios, Theos*, Peru, Illinois: Open Court Publishing Co., 1992.

2. Ibid., 139.

munity and by the scientific community."[3] The ASA has grown to over 2,000 members and subscribers, and there are also significant numbers of members in related organizations internationally in countries such as Canada and the United Kingdom. These are all professing Christians and do not include the multitude of people who believe in an intelligent designer or creator but who are not Christians.

The ASA publishes a sophisticated quarterly journal, *Perspectives on Science and Christian Faith*. The journal has over 300 libraries in the United States and internationally that are subscribers. The ASA also makes available on the Internet "a series of papers on basic science/faith themes designed for the lay reader and students. These are meant to provide material relating aspects of science to the Christian faith to a broad audience. These articles are not meant to be just for scholars but for students, teachers, church leaders, and others who may be interested in these faith/science questions."[4]

LONG-TIME ATHEIST BECOMES A DEIST

An interesting sidelight is the alteration of the beliefs of Dr. Antony Flew, a legendary British philosopher and atheist. For many decades, Dr. Flew had been one of the foremost proponents and spokesmen for atheism. In *Cosmos, Bios, Theos*, Part Three, there is a debate on the subject, titled, "The Existence of God and the Origin of the Universe."[5] Prof. H. D. Lewis defended the position for a creator, while Dr. Flew spoke for the atheistic position. Flew has been a prolific author who argued against the existence of God for more than 50 years.

In an amazing turnabout after all those years as an atheist, Dr. Flew changed his position and now considers himself a deist—a person who believes that God created the universe. On December 10, 2004, the Associated Press reported, "A British Professor who's been a leading champion of atheism for more than 50 years has changed his mind.[6] Antony Flew says scientific evidence has now convinced him that a super-intelligence is the only explanation for the origin of life and the complexity

3. American Scientific Affiliation, www.ASA3.org.

4. Ibid.,

5. Ibid., *Margenau*, 225.

6. Richard N. Ostling, New York: Associated Press, December 10, 2004. Used with permission of The Associated Press Copyright© 2008. All rights reserved.

of nature. Flew says biologists' studies of DNA have shown 'the almost unbelievable complexity of the arrangements needed to produce life. The then 81-year-old Flew says he still doesn't believe in a God that's actively involved in people's lives, but adds, 'It could be a person in the sense of a being that has intelligence and a purpose.' If his newfound belief upsets people, Flew says 'that's too bad'—but he's always been determined to 'follow the evidence wherever it leads.'" In an article in the Baptist Press, Flew states he also believes that Christians are intellectually justified in holding to their religion and that the resurrection of Jesus has more evidential support than any other reported miracle in history.[7]

QUESTIONING EVOLUTION WITHOUT A CREATOR

Why has this situation come about? Over recent decades, scientific endeavors have produced more and more experimental data supporting the concept of intelligent design. More and more scientists have called into question the idea that an undirected spontaneous evolutionary process took place. Many of these scientists do not have a religious "ax to grind." Many of them are not Christians; they are merely seeking the truth, and the holes in the undirected evolutionary process are enormous. I will describe here merely a few factors that point to intelligent design, and where there is intelligent design, there is a designer, or as I prefer, a creator.

Many years ago, there were a number of theories for the initiation and development of the universe. Some theories were variations of the steady state theory in which the universe alternatively contracted and expanded without a beginning. If this condition were true, there would be no indication of a time of creation; ergo, no need for a creator. For many years, this was a favorite theory among those who were biased against intelligent design.

A competing theory proposed the universe started from a beginning, or "Big Bang." Over recent decades, a preponderance of evidence has been emerging to support the "Big Bang," it is now the predominant theory. Among the many supporting experiments, Dr. Arno Penzias and Dr. Robert Wilson of Bell Telephone Laboratories, where I was also employed for a number of years, conducted the one that was the most definitive. Earlier, other cosmologists had proposed that if there were a

---

7. David Roach, *Famed Atheist Admits Evidence for God,* Baptist Press, reprinted in Christian Examiner, January, 2005. Used with permission from the Baptist Press.

"Big Bang," there would be microwave radiation measuring about three degrees Kelvin. Penzias and Wilson were making measurements for other purposes when they came upon background radiation measuring three degrees Kelvin. It was realized they had stumbled upon the single most important discovery confirming the primordial "Big Bang" explosion.[8] In 1978, they were awarded the Nobel Prize for their discovery.

Penzias, in an essay written for *Cosmos, Bios, Theos*, makes an interesting comment about scientists and others who do not accept the concept of a creator: "Well, today's dogma holds that matter is eternal. The dogma comes from the intuitive belief of people (including the majority of physicists) who don't want to accept the observational evidence that the universe was created, despite the fact that the creation of the universe is supported by all the observable data astronomy has produced so far. As a result, the people who reject the data can arguably be described as having a 'religious belief' that matter must be eternal."[9]

In Dr. Jonathan Wells' book, *Icons of Evolution, Science or Myth*, subtitled, *Why much of what we teach about evolution is wrong*, he lists ten reasons for accepting evolution that over the years have been given as factual.[10] Examples include the Miller-Urey experiments on generating amino acids in the laboratory, Darwin's tree of life, Haeckel's embryos, Archaeopterix, the missing link, etc. He refers to these topics as "icons of evolution." In other words, these are many of the pillars on which the theory of creator-less evolution is based. Wells shows how each icon or pillar has crumbled in recent decades, including some in which fraudulent practices have been involved. Dr. Wells holds two Ph.D.s, one of them in molecular and cell biology. He is now a senior fellow at the Discovery Institute's Center for the Renewal of Science and Culture in Seattle.

Another significant factor that raises questions about evolution is the complexity of the human body. In his book, *Evolution: Possible or Impossible?*[11] Dr. James Coppedge, director of the Center for Probability Research in Biology in California, calculated the probability of a single

8. Barry R. Parker, *The Vindication of the Big Bang: Breakthroughs and Barriers,* New York: Plenum Press, 1993.

9. Ibid., Margenau, 79.

10. Dr. Jonathan Wells, *Icons of Evolution,* Washington, D.C.: Regnery Publishing, Inc., 2000.

11. Dr. J. F. Coppedge, *Evolution: Possible or Impossible*? Grand Rapids: Zondervan Publishing House, 1973.

protein molecule being generated by chance. His computation requires 10^{262} (10 multiplied by itself 262 times!) years for a single molecule, a number beyond comprehension.

The uniqueness of the earth in sustaining life is another important consideration. At one time, it was thought the earth was quite ordinary in an ordinary galaxy. Many felt that life was likely throughout the universe. However, this view has also changed. Small modifications in any one of a large number of factors, such as the mass and size of the earth, the tilt of the earth's axis, the presence of the moon, the atmosphere, water, the ozone layer, etc., would render the earth uninhabitable.[12]

ERRORS IN EDUCATION

In light of the above picture of problems with evolution, one may wonder why evolution is still taught as a fact, and not as a controversial theory in schools and universities. Why are they still using antiquated textbooks that promote an undirected evolution as a fact? In my opinion, it is because so many teachers and persons who are involved in generating or approving textbooks have a strong "faith" in an undirected evolution. Moreover, it is difficult for people, including teachers and media journalists, who are not involved in cosmology, biology, paleontology, etc. to keep up with the latest scientific findings. As a result, many individuals over the years have been influenced in their educations to believe that evolution without a creator is a fact. This fallacy has devastated religious beliefs in enormous numbers of people.

Especially apropos to the situation in education is an article in the San Francisco Chronicle, headlined, *Teaching Evolution as Theory not Fact*.[13] The sub-heading was, "Intelligent design booster speaks out." The booster referred to was Professor Phillip Johnson of the University of California at Berkeley.

As indicated in the article, Professor Johnson "does not oppose teaching evolution, but he says it should be presented as a theory not supported by scientific evidence." He is quoted as saying, "Just teach evolution with a recognition that it's controversial." He goes on to say, "The cell is a

---

12. Prof. Peter D. Ward and Prof. Donald Brownlee, *Rare Earth*, New York: Springer-Verlag, 2003.

13. Charles Burress, *Teaching Evolution as Theory not Fact*, San Francisco Chronicle, December 12, 2004.

masterpiece of miniaturized complexity that makes a spaceship or super computer look rather low-tech by comparison. From this we know it is not reasonable to believe that you can produce this quantity and quality of information from random means. Complex, specified information is something which in our experience is produced only by intelligence."

Johnson is also concerned about the teaching of intelligent design as an alternative to Darwinism. He states, "It's the problem of stirring up the automatic reaction from the lobbies that exist to protect Darwinism and have great influence with the media. You get this 'religious fanatics are trying to censor science again' kind of coverage."

Professor Johnson's concern about reactions has proved to be prescient. On October 18, 2004, the Dover, Pennsylvania, school board voted 6–3 to add the teaching of intelligent design to its ninth-grade biology curricula. There is no reference in the curricula as to who the designer may be. However, it has been reported that the American Civil Liberties Union is lodging a lawsuit to eliminate such teaching on the grounds that it is religious in nature.[14] So, another reason for the lack of objectivity in teaching is that powerful forces, such as the ACLU, fiercely oppose such teaching because of their fear that religion is being promoted, even when there is no intent to do so.

As a final comment on the state of the evolutionary theory, evolutionary paleoanthropologist Professor F. Clark Howell, University of California, concedes, "There is no encompassing theory of [human] evolution. Alas, there never really has been."[15]

RECOMMENDED READING

Dr. Hugh Ross, a cosmologist, has written a number of excellent books about creation. A few of them are listed here:

Dr. Hugh Ross, *Creator and the Cosmos*, Colorado Springs: NavPress, 1993.

Dr. Hugh Ross, *Creation and Time*, Colorado Springs: NavPress, 1994.

Dr. Hugh Ross, *Beyond the Cosmos*, Colorado Springs: NavPress, 1996.

Dr. Michael Behe's biochemical challenge to evolution:

Dr. Michael J. Behe, *Darwin's Black Box*, New York: The Free Press, 1996.

Lee Strobel, a former atheist has written a number of books apropos to the subjects in my book. A few of them are listed here:

14. WorldNetDaily, December 14, 2004.

15. Quoted in Lee Strobel, *The Case for a Creator*, Grand Rapids, MI: Zondervan Publishing House, 2004, 64.

Lee Strobel, *The Case for Christ*, Grand Rapids, MI: Zondervan Publishing House, 1998.

Lee Strobel, *The Case for Faith*, Grand Rapids, MI: Zondervan Publishing House, 2000.

Lee Strobel, *The Case for a Creator*, Grand Rapids, MI: Zondervan Publishing House, 2004.

Dr. J. F. Coppedge, *Evolution: Possible or Impossible*? Grand Rapids, MI: Zondervan Publishing House, 1973.

Prof. Peter D. Ward and Prof. Donald Brownlee, *Rare Earth*, New York: Springer-Verlag, 2003.

Dr. Jonathan Wells, *Icons of Evolution*, Washington, DC: Regnery Publishing, Inc., 2000.

Part Two
You Mean He Left Us with a Manual?

2

The Case for the Bible

There is not a righteous man on earth who does what is right and never sins.

Ecclesiastes 7:20

All have sinned and fall short of the glory of God.

Romans 3:23

IDENTIFYING THE MANUAL

A T THIS POINT, I hope all readers accept the logic of the existence of a creator. Unfortunately, some will not. Geisler and Turek point out, "While some faith is required for our conclusions, it's often forgotten that faith is also required to believe any worldview, including atheism and pantheism." Turek can state this premise with some authority, as he was at one time a skeptic.[1] Many will cling to atheism or agnosticism because they simply do not want to believe in God in spite of evidence for a creator. For them, no degree of evidence is adequate. After all, it conflicts with their faith of many years. For some, change is hard.

However, there are large numbers of people who are open to change. They merely need to be exposed to the credible evidence. As discussed earlier, even the noted atheist of decades, Dr. Flew, changed his mind under the weight of overwhelming evidence. His objectivity led him to adjust his thinking. For those of you who are still open to a creator, the

---

1. Norman L. Geisler and F. Turek, *I Don't Have Enough Faith to Be an Atheist*, Wheaton, IL: Crossway Books, 2004, 25.

13

evidence that will unfold in this book should lead you to appropriate decisions for your belief system.

The next step, now that we have a strong case for a creator, is to consider whether or not the creator left us with a "manual" or guidebook for living. Is it logical that the creator would leave us without any communication from him as to how we should relate to him and conduct our lives? After all, we are a people of communications. If we are to behave according to his principles, how do we do that without knowing those principles?

OTHER RELIGIOUS DOCUMENTS

Unfortunately, there are numerous religions claiming they have the one true document from God. With the exception of the Bible, most of the others have similarities. Typically, they are written by one person, such as the Koran, written by Muhammad. Or, they have been received by one person, presumably from God or an angel, such as the golden plates received by Joseph Smith of the Church of Latter Day Saints. These plates are no longer in evidence. Another similarity is that man must work for his "salvation." He must endeavor to improve his character. In the final analysis, if his good works outweigh his evil deeds, God will accept him into heaven. In at least one religion, and also believed by many individuals, "all roads lead to God." In other words, all beliefs are acceptable to God, even though they conflict with each other in major ways. Another major differential with the Biblical God is the idea that the creator has no involvement with his creation. For example, one of the five articles of faith of Islam declares, "There is only one true God and his name is Allah. Allah is all knowing, all-powerful and the sovereign judge. *Yet Allah is not a personal God, for he is so far above man in every way that he is not personally knowable* (emphasis added).[2] McDowell and Stewart also state, "The emphasis of the God of Islam is on judgment, not grace; on power, not mercy. He is the source of both good and evil and his will is supreme."[3] I do not wish to single out Islam, and although it is unpopular to be critical of other beliefs, all non-Biblical religions have flawed views. These views may be described as "creating God in man's image," instead

2. Josh McDowell and D. Stewart, *Handbook of Today's Religions*, Nashville: Thomas Nelson Publishers, 1983, 389.

3. Ibid.

of the Biblical view, in which God creates us in his image. In these cases, men have decided what God is like and what his standards are; therefore, it must be so. If the God of the Bible does not match up to these standards, he is rejected. Contrast these views with those of the God of the Bible: loving, yet righteous; personal, not remote; merciful, not hateful. His plan of salvation does not involve works, but accepting his gift of grace: accepting Jesus Christ as Savior leading to eternal life with him. I shall expound on this principle in chapter seven.

HOW IS THE GOD OF THE BIBLE DIFFERENT? GOD THE COMMUNICATOR

Unlike the god of some other religions, the God of the Bible is active throughout all the centuries since creation. He has been a communicator throughout all time. In many periods of the Old Testament, God has spoken directly to his people. As early as the Garden of Eden, we find God communicating directly with Adam and Eve (Genesis 2 and 3). A few chapters later in chapters six through nine, he talks to Noah and gives him the directions for constructing the ark. He tells Noah how to go about the collection of the animals. After the flood subsides, he makes a personal covenant with Noah and his descendants.

Other instances of God communicating directly with man take place with Abraham (Genesis 12:1–3; 17:22), Jacob (Genesis 31:3), Moses (Exodus 32:7–10), the prophet Samuel (1 Samuel 3:4–14), the prophet Nathan (2 Samuel 7:4–17), Job (Job 38:1—41:34), and Saul before he became the Apostle Paul (Acts 9:4–6). These are just a few examples, as there are many other direct conversations with God.

Through Angels

Another way in which God communicates is through angels. Throughout the Bible we see that one of the primary tasks of angels is to convey messages from God. For example, when God sent angels to destroy Sodom in Genesis 19, the angels told Lot, Abraham's nephew, to flee with his family before the destruction was about to fall upon the city. It was an angel the Lord used to announce to shepherds the birth of Jesus: "Do not be afraid; for behold, I bring you good news of a great joy which shall be for all the people; for today in the city of David there has been born for you a Savior, who is Christ the Lord" (Luke 2:9–12). In another instance, Herod was about to destroy all male children under the age of two to eliminate the competition of the future king of the Jews. An angel appeared to Joseph in a dream and told him, "Arise and take the child and his mother, and flee to Egypt, and remain there until I tell you; for Herod is going to search for the child to destroy him" (Matthew 2:13).

Through "His Angel" or the "Angel of the Lord"

In some cases, it appears that God himself has appeared as an angel in an interaction with a human being. When Sarah's handmaiden, Hagar, became pregnant by Abraham, Hagar fled in fear. An "angel of the Lord" spoke to her, and told her to return and that she would be safe. He prophesied she would have a son whom she would name Ishmael, declaring, "His hand will be against everyone, and everyone's hand will be against him" (Genesis 16:12). Hagar believed the angel was God: "Then she called the name of the Lord *who spoke to her* (emphasis added), 'Thou art a God who sees;' for she said, 'Have I even remained alive here after seeing him?'" (Genesis 16:13).

Another instance took place after Ishmael was a teenager and Isaac had been born to Abraham and Sarah. Abraham sent Hagar and Ishmael away at Sarah's urging. In desperation, when Hagar and Ishmael were out of water and it appeared they would die, she cried out to God. "And God heard the lad crying; and the *angel of God* (emphasis added) called to Hagar from Heaven, and said to her, 'What is the matter with you, Hagar? Do not fear, for God has heard the voice of the lad where he is. Arise, lift up the lad, and hold him by the hand; for I will make a great nation of him.' Then *God* (emphasis added) opened her eyes and she saw a well of water; and she went and filled the skin with water, and gave the lad a drink" (Genesis 21:17–19).

In another incident, when God recruited Gideon to lead a battle against the Midianites, the Bible states, "When the *angel of the Lord* (emphasis added) appeared to him and said to him, 'The Lord is with you, O mighty warrior.'" Then it reads, "And the *Lord turned to him and said* (emphasis added), 'Go in the strength you have and save Israel out of Midian's hand. Am I not sending you?'" (Judges 6:12–14). As with the other two instances above, the angel of the Lord (or of God) may refer to God himself.

Dreams and Visions

God spoke to many in the Bible through dreams and visions. We saw that God's angel appeared to Joseph in a dream to warn him of Herod's perfidy and to protect the baby Jesus. In the Old Testament, God often communicated through dreams and visions. In a dynamic story of God's sovereignty, Nebuchadnezzar, king of Babylon, had a frightening dream from God. He called upon his wise men to tell him what he had dreamed and what was the interpretation. Of course, they were unable to give him an interpretation without knowing the dream's content. Nebuchadnezzar ordered all the wise men of the kingdom to be put to death. However, God revealed to his prophet Daniel in a vision the meaning of the dream, which had to do with a prophecy of the succession of the kingdoms of Medo-Persia, Greece, and Rome. The king's reaction was dramatic: "Then King Nebuchadnezzar fell prostrate before Daniel and paid him honor and ordered that an offering and incense be presented to him. The king said to Daniel, 'Surely your God is the God of gods and the Lord of kings and a revealer of mysteries, for you were able to reveal this mystery'" (Daniel 2:46–47). The king then made Daniel the ruler of the whole province.

Through the Prophets

As were the angels, prophets were messengers of God. Although the common understanding of prophecy is foretelling the future, this type of prophecy is actually a subset of the broader meaning of bringing a message from God. The primary role of prophets was to convey God's instructions. All throughout the Bible, God utilized prophets to communicate with his people. All through the Old Testament, prophets were available to Israel. As early as the book of Exodus (the second book of the Bible), Moses brought the law and God's direction to the people. Until Jesus Christ, there was no prophet the likes of Moses (Deuteronomy 34:10–12). Many others, such as Joshua, Samuel, Nathan, Elijah, Isaiah, Jeremiah, Ezekiel, etc., followed Moses. Even the Israelites in exile in Assyria and Babylon had prophets to instruct them. The form of the message varied widely; however, the message from God often was in the following form: "If you do what I instruct, you will be blessed. If you do not, there will be negative consequences." For example, in 2 Chronicles 7:14, God states, "If my people, who are called by my name, will humble themselves and pray and seek my face and turn from their wicked ways, then will I hear from heaven and will forgive their sin and will heal their land."

In the New Testament, John the Baptist continued the tradition. However, as deliverers of God's word, all of the writers of the Bible were prophets. The Bible tells us Jesus was the greatest of the prophets. As stated in Hebrews 1:1–2, "In the past, God spoke to our forefathers through the prophets at many times and in various ways, but in these last days he has spoken to us by his Son, whom he appointed heir of all things, and through whom he made the universe." In chapter three, I will detail many of the prophecies that had to do with the foretelling of the future, specifically about the many aspects of the Messiah to come, Jesus Christ.

Through Inspiration

An important premise of this work is that the Bible is the word of God. At this point, the premise may seem to be circular reasoning. The rest of this chapter and other chapters to follow will show evidence for the uniqueness of the Bible. In ancient times, God had chosen many unique ways to communicate with his created beings for specific historical events. Over a long period, authors who were inspired by the Holy Spirit wrote the books of the Bible. It was God's plan to leave us with the Bible, which has endured as his continuing message to mankind, to all who would seek him and wish to know what his will is for all creation. It is amazing that its tenets have held for centuries.

The apostle Paul relates in 2 Timothy 3:16–19, "All Scripture is God-breathed and is useful for teaching, rebuking, correcting and training in righteousness, so that the man of God may be thoroughly equipped for every good work." This verse is so pertinent that I used it at the top of this chapter. God-breathed may also be translated as "inspiration." Inspiration does not imply dictation. However, as I have personally experienced in this work, I believe God places thoughts into men's minds as a form of communication. God is an all-powerful, sovereign, God. While one may feel that such actions are extraordinary or difficult to believe, they are child's play to the sovereign God, the creator of the universe. The result is a coherent body of work from Genesis to Revelation that God intended for communication with his creation. I will present more information on this topic in chapter six.

STRUCTURE OF THE BIBLE

The Christian Bible, both Protestant and Roman Catholic versions, consists of two major sections, the Old Testament and the New Testament. There are some other variations between Protestant and Catholic versions in the particular books that are included. The Hebrew Bible contains only the Old Testament. At the time of Jesus, only the Old Testament was extant, and was frequently referred to by Jesus and the New Testament authors, as "The Scriptures." Moreover, the word "testament" is better rendered "covenant," according to the Greek.[4] Therefore, we may think of these major sections as delineating our covenants with God.

The Bible was written over a range of centuries. It is comprised of 66 books by over 40 different authors inspired by the Holy Spirit. It was written in 3 languages, Hebrew, Greek, and Aramaic, on 3 continents. The writings cover a 1500-year time span, and as aptly stated by Morley, "These included kings and peasants, philosophers and fishermen, poets and statesmen, shepherds and soldiers. Even with such remarkable diversity, the Scriptures by far possess the greatest unity and continuity among the great works of literature." Morley goes on to say, "Whereas only five complete manuscripts of Aristotle and twelve of Plato exist, thirteen thousand New Testament manuscripts have survived the centuries."[5]

The Old Testament, or the Hebrew Bible, is comprised of 39 books. The structure takes the form, 5–12–5–5–12. The first five stands for the five books of law, which are known as the Pentateuch (Greek) or The Torah (Hebrew). It is generally accepted by Jewish and Christian scholars that Moses authored or compiled The Torah. While the writing of the Torah by Moses is considered to have occurred circa 1446 BC, it covers an enormous period of time beginning with the creation process: "In the beginning, God created the heavens and the earth" (Genesis 1:1). It ends during Moses' lifetime with the writing of the book of Deuteronomy, or somewhat before 1500 BC. The historical period of Moses' life can be fixed with a fair degree of accuracy by the book of 1 Kings.[6] The Pentateuch or Torah is followed by twelve books of history, five books of poetry or wis-

---

4. Walter A. Ewell, Ph.D. and P. W. Comfort, Ph.D., Editors, *Tyndale Bible Dictionary,* Wheaton, IL: Tyndale House Publishers, 2001, 168.

5. Patrick Morley, *Devotions for the Man in the Mirror,* Grand Rapids: Zondervan, 1998, 130.

6. Kenneth Barker, Ed., *The NIV Study Bible,* Grand Rapids: Zondervan, 1995, 2.

dom literature, five major prophets, and twelve minor prophets. Because the Torah contains a great deal of history, it is sometimes grouped with the 12 books of history.

The New Testament is comprised of 27 books, all written by persons who lived during Christ's lifetime and who witnessed the events that took place. Most of them were apostles who had been trained directly by Jesus. I shall give more details on some of these apostles in chapter eight on transformed lives. The New Testament begins with the four gospels, depicting Jesus' life, crucifixion, resurrection, and ascension. The gospels are followed by the book of Acts, detailing the founding of the church and its spread throughout the Mediterranean lands. The next 13 books are letters to the churches, written by the apostle Paul, followed by the "general epistles," written by other apostles. The New Testament concludes with the book of Revelation, written by the apostle John.

With such a profusion of authors, locations, and backgrounds, it is amazing there is such a unified story throughout. How can this be? To me, there is one explanation, accepted by Biblical authorities and the everyday believer: inspiration by the Holy Spirit. As expressed by the apostle Paul in 1 Corinthians, "However, as it is written: 'No eye has seen, no ear has heard, no mind has conceived what God has prepared for those who love him,' but God has revealed it to us by his Spirit" (1 Corinthians 2:9–13). There is no other religious document that even approaches the number of authors that have contributed to the Bible. It is much more consistent with a God who can inspire many authors to write a unified story than the singular authors of other religions.

HISTORICITY

Historicity refers to historical accuracy. It requires that any and all facts in the Bible that can be examined historically must be true. This is especially important for the Bible, because it was written so long ago. Unlike the documents of the other religions, the Bible consists of 66 separate books and was written by over 40 authors. The earliest writings date from before 1500 BC, and they cover a period of authorship of about 1100 years. Do they agree with one another? Are the New Testament and Old Testament writings consistent? Many details on the subject of consistency are presented in chapter six. In the next few sections, I address the issue of historicity.

Sources

Since there are no originals that have been discovered, it is important to consider the sources that have led to the translations that we use throughout Judaism and Christendom. The sources were typically handwritten scrolls on a number of materials, such as papyrus or animal skins. Modern discoveries have yielded many thousands of manuscripts. In a Cairo synagogue, some 200,000 fragments were found, many of them from the Bible.[7]

Over many centuries, a number of versions of the Scriptures had been assembled, some in widely separated areas. During this time, faithful scribes copied the writings over and over again to make them available to clergy and worshippers. According to F.E. Peters, "On the basis of manuscript tradition alone, the works that made up the Christians' New Testament were the most frequently copied and widely circulated books of antiquity."[8] Copies were distributed in all directions over the ancient world. How did they remain so accurate?

Large collections of manuscripts are spread all over the world in places such as Leningrad, the British Museum, New York, and many more locations. Because the scribes were believers and revered the materials they were working from and generating, the writings were treated with great reverence and care. The world owes a great debt to these caretakers of the manuscripts over so many centuries. The Hebrew Bible has been handed down through the efforts of a succession of scholars whose responsibility it was in maintaining accuracy from the earliest days of their efforts going back to the second and first centuries before Christ.[9] According to McDowell, "The Masoretes were the Jewish scholars who between A.D. 500 and A.D. 950 gave the final form to the text of the Old Testament." This document became known as the Masoretic Text, which is still one of the primary editions of the Old Testament. There also were other scriptural lines such as the well-known Septuagint, the Samaritan Pentateuch, and others. Amazingly, the agreement within these separate lines is excellent. As an affirmation of the accuracy of these ancient manuscripts and the resulting canons, Professor Wilson has remarked, "that the

7. Josh McDowell, *The New Evidence That Demands a Verdict,* Nashville: Thomas Nelson Publishers,1999, 72.

8. Peters, quoted in Ibid., 34.

9. Ibid., 73.

Hebrew text should have been transmitted by copyists through so many centuries is a phenomenon unequaled in the history of literature."[10]

Although the agreement among the various lines of scripture was amazing, there was a bothersome factor until the discovery of the Dead Sea Scrolls in 1947 by a Bedouin boy. Until that time the oldest Masoretic Old Testament text was from the tenth century A.D. The Dead Sea Scrolls yielded some 40,000 fragments, from which more than 500 books have been assembled.[11] These scrolls included copies of the Old Testament dating from more than 100 years before Christ. One of the caves contained New Testament fragments dating as early as A.D. 50 or 60. These are very important, as some critics had claimed the New Testament writings occurred much later. Another important finding was that the scroll of the book Isaiah was essentially identical to the 1000-year younger Masoretic text. This finding vindicated the validity of Isaiah 53. The picture this chapter presents of Jesus Christ as Messiah is so comprehensive that the critics said it surely had to have been written after the time of Christ. Once again, the critics were proven to be wrong. In fact, in a comparison of the Dead Sea Scrolls and the Masoretic Text, McDowell states, "There is a word-for-word identity in more than 95 percent of the cases, and the 5-percent variation consists mostly of slips of the pen and spelling." This is amazing agreement for documents that are 1000 years different in age!

As for the New Testament, there is a wealth of manuscripts and fragments of manuscripts. According to McDowell, "There are now more then 5,686 known Greek manuscripts of the New Testament. Add over 10,000 Latin Vulgate and at least 9,300 other early versions, and we have close to if not more than, 25,000 manuscript copies of portions of the New Testament in existence today. No other document of antiquity even begins to approach such numbers and attestation. In comparison, Homer's *Iliad* is second, with only 643 manuscripts that still survive. The first complete preserved text of Homer dates from the thirteenth century."[12] McDowell continues, "John Warwick Montgomery says that 'to be skeptical of the resultant text of the New Testament books is to allow all of classical antiquity to slip into obscurity, for no documents of the ancient period are

---

10. Ibid., 70.
11. Ibid., 77.
12. Ibid., 84.

as well attested bibliographically as the New Testament."[13] McDowell concludes, "One problem that I constantly face is the desire on the part of many to apply one standard or test to secular literature and another to the Bible. One must apply the same test, whether the literature under investigation is secular or religious."

Evidence for the validity of the existing manuscripts comes from a variety of sources. First of all, the New Testament writers themselves and Jesus often referred to, and quoted from, the "Scriptures." The Scriptures were the books of the Hebrew Bible. I will just give a few examples here, as I will cover this subject in chapter six, *Consistency Between the Old and New Testaments*. In 2 Timothy 3:16–17, the Apostle Paul says, "All Scripture is God-breathed and is useful for teaching, rebuking, correcting and training in righteousness, so that the man of God may be thoroughly equipped for every good work." The Apostle Peter has similar words about the Scriptures in 2 Peter 1:20–21, "Above all, you must understand that no prophecy of Scripture came about by the prophet's own interpretation. For prophecy never had its origin in the will of man, but men spoke from God as they were carried along by the Holy Spirit." Each of these verses has great wisdom, but just as important, they show the reverence that each of these apostles had for the Scriptures. Equally significant, the authors had reverence for their peers' writings. In the same letter of Peter that I just quoted, he says of Paul's teaching, "Bear in mind that our Lord's patience means salvation, just as our dear brother Paul also wrote you with the wisdom that God gave him" (2 Peter 3:15).

Church Fathers

It is clear the early church fathers not only had many of the New Testament documents available to them, but they used them extensively in widely different geographical arenas. Eusebius, Papias, Irenaeus, Clement of Rome, Ignatius, and Polycarp are typical of the early fathers who quoted liberally from the New Testament in their books, sermons, commentaries, and other first and second century works. Why is this important? After all they were leaders of the early church. As Geisler affirms, "First, they give overwhelming support to the existence of the twenty-seven books of the New Testament canon. Second, the quotations are so numerous and widespread that if no manuscripts of the New Testament were extant,

---

13. Montgomery, quoted in Ibid., 35.

the New Testament could be reproduced from the writings of the early Fathers alone."[14] Geisler is not alone in his comments. Other historians have made nearly identical statements.

Non-Believer Comments

The quotations by early church fathers are certainly not surprising, but are indications of the extensive availability of the manuscripts. However, also of importance are the references by non-believer historians who by their writings affirm the occurrence of events, existence of individuals, and verify locations in the Scriptures. For example, Tacitus, a Roman is "considered one of the more accurate historians of the ancient world." In his description of the fire of Rome, he refers to Christians and talks about an individual, Christus, who "suffered the extreme penalty during the reign of Tiberius at the hands of one of our procurators, Pontius Pilate."[15] Here we have unbiased evidence of the crucifixion of Christ.

Another very important documenter of first century events was Josephus. He was a Pharisee and Jewish historian and not a Christian believer. In his writings on the Old Testament, "He even lists the names of the books, which are identical with the thirty-nine books of the Protestant Old Testament."[16] Also very important is Josephus' documentation of the existence of the prophet Daniel, establishing his presence at a time well before the outcome of Daniel's greatest prophecies. Josephus also made references to many New Testament individuals such as John the Baptist and James, the brother of Jesus, describing events in their lives that are consistent with the New Testament. Josephus further attests, "Now there was about this time, a wise man, if it be lawful to call him a man, for he was a doer of wonderful works, a teacher of such men as receive the truth with pleasure. He drew over to him both many of the Jews and many of the Gentiles. He was [the] Christ; and when Pilate, at the suggestion of the principal men amongst us, had condemned him to the cross, those that loved him at the first did not forsake him. For he appeared to them alive again on the third day, as the divine prophets had foretold these and ten thousand other wonderful things concerning him; and the tribe of

---

14. Geisler, quoted in Ibid., 42–43.

15. McDowell, Ibid., 55.

16. Ibid., 56.

Christians, so named from him, are not extinct to this day."[17] And this from a non-believer!

Archaeology

Why is archaeology important? It is because archaeology is a continuing source of new information about antiquity. A branch of archaeology, Biblical archaeology, gives us information about the validity of the people, locations, events, etc. in the Bible. It is especially of interest because there have been so many critics who not only rejected miracles and any "supernatural" events, but also denied the existence of many Biblical historical accounts. I have already detailed above the significance of the findings of the Dead Sea Scrolls. While these discoveries were of utmost importance, there have also been many other archaeological findings that have supported the Bible.

According to McDowell, "In the nineteenth and twentieth centuries, the Bible took a beating from higher criticism. Critics have sought to destroy the foundations of the historicity of the Bible by showing that the Bible has errors and must be adjusted to fit the 'facts' of archaeology. But now the tables are turning."[18] McDowell also states, "A substantial proof for the accuracy of the Old Testament text has come from archaeology. Numerous discoveries have confirmed the historical accuracy of the biblical documents, even down to the occasional use of obsolete names of foreign kings. These archaeological confirmations of the accuracy of Scripture have been recorded in numerous books."

At this point, I will mention just a few examples where archaeology has provided substantiation of biblical accounts. The Apostle Luke had frequently been cited by critics as being inaccurate. In Luke 2:1–3, he states, "In those days Caesar Augustus issued a decree that a census should be taken of the entire Roman world. (This was the first census that took place while Quirinius was governor of Syria.) And everyone went to his own town to register." Every fact in these few verses were declared untrue by critics at various times in the past. However, archaeology came to the rescue. "First of all, archaeological discoveries show that the Romans had a regular enrollment of taxpayers and also held censuses every fourteen years. . . . Second, we find evidence that Quirinius was governor of Syria

17. Flavius Josephus, *Antiquities of the Jews*, xvii 3.3.
18. McDowell, Ibid., 91.

around 7 B.C. . . . Last, in regard to the practices of enrollment, a papyrus found in Egypt gives directions for the conduct of a census."[19] The latter document indicated that all who were away from their homes had to return. Ergo, Luke was completely vindicated in every detail. In addition, many other criticisms of Luke's writings have been turned over by archaeological findings.

Another controversial Biblical account is the story of the walls of Jericho—a favorite target of critics. McDowell tells us, " During the excavations of Jericho (1930–1936) Garstang found something so startling that he and two other members of the team prepared and signed a statement describing what was found." McDowell continues with a comment from Garstang: "As to the main fact, then, there remains no doubt: the walls fell outwards so completely that the attackers would be able to clamber up and over their ruins into the city. Why so unusual? Because the walls of cities do not fall outwards, they fall inwards."[20] What does the Bible say? "and the wall fell down flat, so that the people went up into the city, every man straight before him, and they took the city." It was just as Garsang found it to be—over 3,000 years after the book of Joshua was written!

There were many other criticisms about numerous situations beyond the scope of this book. In David's capture of Jerusalem, there were doubts about the Biblical passage that describes an entry via a water tunnel. There were doubts about the existence of Sargon, Belshazzar, the Hittites, and others. Archaeology proved the critics wrong in every one of these and a myriad of other cases. Archaeologist and Reformed Jewish scholar Nelson Glueck asserts, "It may be stated categorically that no archaeological discovery has ever controverted a Biblical reference. Scores of archaeological findings have been made which confirm in clear outline or exact detail historical statements in the Bible."[21] Critical tradition held that as archaeological discoveries would provide more and more evidence, the Bible would be shown to be incorrect in many details. The reverse has occurred. Scholars have had to admit they were incorrect in their criticisms of the Bible. One may conclude that the historicity of the Bible cannot be denied thus far, on the basis of archaeological findings. For more in-depth studies, please see the recommended readings at the end of the chapter.

19. Ibid., 63.

20. Garstang, quoted in Ibid., 95.

21. Glueck, quoted in Ibid., 89.

RECOMMENDED READING

Arthur G. Patzia, *The Making of the New Testament,* Downers Grove, IL: Intervarsity Press, 1995.

Norman L Geisler and Frank Turek, *I Don't Have Enough Faith to Be an Atheist,* Wheaton, IL: Crossway Books, 2004.

Josh McDowell and Don Stewart, *Handbook of Today's Religions,* Nashville: Thomas Nelson Publishers, 1983.

Josh McDowell, *The New Evidence That Demands a Verdict,* Nashville: Thomas Nelson Publishers, 1999.

Joseph P. Free and Howard F. Vos, *Archaeology and Bible History,* Grand Rapids, MI: Zondervan Publishing House, 1992.

Keith N. Schoville, *Biblical Archaeology in Focus,* Grand Rapids, MI: Baker Book House, 1978.

3

Prophecy Fulfilled

And we have the word of the prophets made more certain, and you will do well to pay attention to it, as to a light shining in a dark place, until the day dawns and the morning star rises in your hearts. Above all, you must understand that no prophecy of Scripture came about by the prophet's own interpretation. For prophecy never had its origin in the will of man, but men spoke from God as they were carried along by the Holy Spirit.

2 Peter 1:19–21

SOME YEARS AGO, THERE was a program on television called *Early Edition*.[1] The basis for the program was that each morning a newspaper was at the door of the apartment of the lead actor of the program. The unique aspect of the newspaper was that it was the next day's edition—it contained tomorrow's news! Fortunately, the hero of the program did not trade stocks or bet on the horses. He headed off injuries, deaths, and other hurtful situations. As he helped people out of their dire situation, the news in the paper changed to reflect the improved circumstances. It was pure fantasy, but it gives us insights into the concept of prophecy. Some power must have had the foreknowledge to issue the unique edition and change the paper as conditions changed.

Similarly, as we explore fulfillments of Biblical prophecies, it attests to the amazing power of the one who was the originator of the prophecies—the Creator, and it affirms the credibility of the scriptures containing the fulfilled prophecies. Only the Bible contains great numbers of fulfilled prophecies. In the appendices of his classical work on prophecy, Walvoord

---

1. Vik Rubenfeld and Pat Page, *Early Edition,* CBS, 1996–2000.

lists over a thousand prophecies from the Old and New Testaments.[2] Most of these prophecies have been fulfilled, while a number await future timeframes, such as the return of Jesus and the end times.

Now, project yourself back to a time before the birth of Jesus Christ. You are a sincere Jew, and you are looking forward to the coming of your Messiah. What would he be like? Where would you go to find out? Well, the Bible of those times, the Old Testament, or as referred to in the New Testament as *The Scriptures*, contained details of what he would be like— just as in *Early Edition*.

Before we explore some of those prophecies, I would like to clarify what prophecy is. Prophecy has two connotations. The first is a message from God; the second meaning implies a prediction of a future event or occurrence. It is the latter meaning upon which we will concentrate. The reason is that if we can show many prophecies in the Bible have come to pass, the Bible's credibility as a divinely inspired document is greatly strengthened. At this point, I introduce what I like to think of as the *salt and pepper principle*. The meaning of this principle is that the Bible does not have a few fulfilled prophecies in one or two locations. Rather, the Bible is salted and peppered with prophecies throughout. In both the Old and New Testaments there are many prophecies that have been fulfilled. Many have been fulfilled in Jesus Christ. Other prophecies are about other individuals or situations, and many remain to be fulfilled in the future. An important point is that if Jesus Christ is not the Messiah, how would we recognize another if he emerged? The fulfilled Messianic prophecies are so specific to Jesus Christ that we could not recognize a different Messiah if he turned up. For example, how would we know if he were from the lineage of David, a requirement for the Messiah?

As mentioned above, there are over one thousand prophecies in the Bible. To expound on many of these prophecies is beyond the scope of this book. However, I do wish to give enough examples that it will be clear that fulfilled prophecies are excellent evidences for the veracity of the Bible. I will first give a few examples from the Old Testament, and then I will go on to discuss many that are specific to the Messiah, Jesus Christ.

---

2. John F. Walvoord, *The Prophecy Knowledge Handbook*, Wheaton: Victor Books, 1990, 647–769.

OLD TESTAMENT

Abraham

The origin of the Israel nation came about when God chose Abraham and made an amazing covenant with him. In Genesis 12:2, we read, "I will make you into a great nation and I will bless you; I will make your name great, and you will be a blessing . . . " This was no casual promise, as God reiterates this covenant in Genesis 18:18 and again in Genesis 22:17. The same promises were made to Abraham's son Isaac in Genesis 26:4 and to Isaac's son Jacob in Genesis 28:13–14.

There can be no question about this covenant and prophecy being fulfilled. Abraham's family expanded into a great nation generations after Abraham's death. Even today, Israel exists as a prophetic nation, preserved under incredible odds and adversity from all of its neighbors. Did God make Abraham's name great? I am sure that in some obscure corners of the earth, he is unknown; but throughout much of the world, his name is considered great. Even Islam reveres him as their forefather. Moreover, Abraham was blessed with great prosperity.

Daniel

There were many great prophets throughout the Old Testament, which includes five books by major prophets and twelve books by minor prophets. Daniel was one of the majors. He was one of a number of the nobility who were conscripted by their Babylonian captors after Israel was given over to Babylonia. Daniel showed a unique ability to interpret dreams, a gift given by God, according to Daniel. When King Nebuchadnezzar had a frightening dream, he called for his large cadre of wise men, magicians, sorcerers, etc. to not only interpret the dream, but also tell him what the dream was all about. None of them was able to tell him what the dream was all about, much less interpret it. He was about to kill all of them. However, as shown in the second chapter of the book of Daniel, it became known that Daniel had exceptional capabilities in this area, and Daniel was brought before the king.

Daniel acknowledged that only God could give one the interpretation of the dream and took no credit for himself. God showed Daniel the dream, which depicted an enormous statue, consisting of various metals and clay. He pointed out that the various parts of the statue represented

Babylonia and the next three kingdoms to come. In Daniel 2:47, we read the words of Nebuchadnezzar, "Surely your God is the God of gods and the Lord of kings and a revealer of mysteries, for you were able to reveal this mystery." History verified the succession of nations as the Medo-Persians, the Greeks, and the Romans. Equally incredible is the prophecy in Daniel 9, in which he predicts events throughout 490 years, depicting the time the Messiah, or Anointed One will come. That time coincides with the birth of Jesus Christ.[3]

David

David was a great king of Israel. Many know the story of how, as a young lad, he defeated the Philistine giant, Goliath. In addition to his prowess as a warrior, he had great faith in God. In fact, it was through that faith he defeated the giant, and later as king, God blessed him with great victories over the enemies of Israel. But why did God bless him? He certainly was not sinless, as evidenced by his adulterous affair with Bathsheba and the murder of her husband. Yet God called him "a man after his own heart." It was because throughout his life David expressed an incredible love for God. The Psalms are replete with his wonderful praises for God, many of them when he was under great duress from his enemies.

As a result, God singled out his lineage to be a dynasty forever, as expressed in 2 Samuel 7. Here God sends the prophet Nathan to David with the following message. In verses 8–9:

> Now then, tell my servant David, "This is what the Lord Almighty says: I took you from the pasture and from following the flock to be ruler over my people Israel. I have been with you wherever you have gone, and I have cut off all your enemies from before you. Now I will make your name great, like the names of the greatest men of the earth."

In verse 16:

> Your house and your kingdom will endure forever before me; your throne will be established forever.

That David was followed by a succession of kings is indicated throughout the historical books of the Old Testament. That his name was made great is not in question. His name and story persists to the present day.

3. Ibid., 134, 248–50.

However, what about the word in this prophecy: *forever*? In the first chapter of Matthew, we have a genealogy recording the progression from David to Jesus Christ. It is clear from many sections of the New Testament that this word refers to the future and eternal kingdom of Jesus Christ. So, in David's dynasty, we have fulfilled prophecies about his name and the kingdoms to follow him. The eternal kingdom of Jesus will be fulfilled in the future.

THE MESSIAH

The Old and New Testaments contain many fulfilled prophecies about the Messiah, and others about His future and eternal kingdom. I have selected some of the key verses that show fulfillment in Jesus Christ. We will note the prophecies about the Messiah's virgin birth, his place of birth, his entry into Jerusalem, his betrayal, that he was to die by crucifixion, and that he was to be raised from the dead. Finally, we will explore one of the most amazing chapters in the Old Testament, Isaiah 53.

The Virgin Birth

The virgin birth is predicted in Isaiah 7:14: "Therefore the Lord himself will give you a sign: The virgin will be with child and will give birth to a Son, and will call him Immanuel." Immanuel means *God with us*, and clearly indicates the Messiah to come. The fulfillment is given in Matt. 1:18–25 and Luke 1:26–38. An angel is sent to Mary and tells her she will have a child through the act of the Holy Spirit. When it is learned she is pregnant, Joseph, to whom she is betrothed, considers a divorce. However, he also receives a visit from an angel who explains the situation, and Joseph goes through with the marriage. The virgin birth is difficult to believe by many persons, sometimes the main barrier to their belief in Jesus as the Son of God. However, when we consider the incredible power of God in creating the universe, is the creation of a baby impossible? An important factor is that both Mary and Joseph are of the lineage of David, necessary to fulfill prophecies about the Messiah.

Place of Birth

We all know that Jesus was born in Bethlehem. Even in secular life we hear about it all through the Christmas season. But how many know the prophet Micah foretold this event over seven centuries before it took place. Micah is one of the twelve books of the *minor prophets*. The term minor prophet is not an indication of lesser importance. Rather, it has to do with these books being shorter in length than the five major prophetic books.

Micah 5:12 reads, "But you, Bethlehem Ephrathah, though you are small among the clans of Judah, out of you will come for me one who will be ruler over Israel, whose origins are from old, from ancient times." When Herod had heard that Magi had come from the east to worship the one who was born king of the Jews, he called the chief priests and teachers of the law to find out what the scriptures said about the prophetic location of the birth of the Christ. They quoted to him the above passage.

But wait a minute. Didn't Joseph's family reside in Nazareth? So how did Jesus get born in Bethlehem? In the second chapter of Luke, we learn that Joseph and the pregnant Mary were indeed in Nazareth. Without an intervention from an unlikely source, Jesus would have been born in Nazareth. We learn in Luke and other secular sources at that particular time, "Caesar Augustus issued a decree that a census should be taken of the entire Roman world." Because Joseph was of the line of David, he had to go to Bethlehem to register. Ergo, Jesus was born on that trip in Bethlehem. After the family registration and the birth of Jesus, the family returned to their home in Nazareth. Now why in the world did Caesar Augustus decide to have a census? Was this decision another case of God using a nonbeliever to bring about his purposes? I certainly believe that was the case, or it was an amazing coincidence.

Entry into Jerusalem

In another of the minor prophets, Zechariah 9:9, we find another prediction about the Messiah. "Rejoice greatly, O daughter of Zion! Shout, Daughter of Jerusalem! See, your king comes to you, righteous and having salvation, gentle and riding on a donkey, on a colt, the foal of a donkey." In all four gospels, we read about the triumphant entry of Jesus into Jerusalem. Indeed, he rode into Jerusalem on a colt of a donkey. The people laid their cloaks and palm branches on the ground before him, shouting praises to the *Son of David*. This event led to the celebration of Palm Sunday, one week before Easter Sunday, by Christians of many denominations.

Betrayal

Psalm 41:9 reads, "Even my close friend, whom I trusted, he who shared my bread, has lifted his heel against me." I admit, taken by itself, this verse could be considered too vague to be a definitive prophecy. However, in John 13:18, Jesus quotes this verse in predicting he will be betrayed: "But this is to fulfill the scripture: 'He who shares my bread has lifted up his heel against me.'" Jesus tells his disciples in all four Gospels he will be betrayed by one of them. In Mathew 26: 25, he specifically identifies Judas. As indicated in all four Gospels, the capture of Jesus was not accomplished without the betrayal by Judas.

To Die by Crucifixion

His death by crucifixion was identified centuries before in the book of Psalms, written by his ancestor, David. In Psalm 22:14–18, many of the elements of crucifixion are identified:

> I am poured out like water, and all my bones are out of joint. My heart has turned to wax; it has melted away within me. My strength is dried up like a potsherd, and my tongue sticks to the roof of my mouth.
> They have pierced my hands and my feet. I can count all my bones; people stare and gloat over me. They divide my garments among them and cast lots for my clothing.

All of these descriptions came to pass on the cross. Even a detail such as the casting of lots for his clothing was fulfilled as described in Matthew 27:35 and John 19:23–24. How could the prophecy about his death centuries earlier be sure that it would be crucifixion? How could it be known that it would be the Romans in power centuries later, a government that utilized crucifixion? Who could be sure the leaders in Jerusalem would incite the crowd to cry out for him to be crucified? Perhaps he could have been hung, or killed by stoning, lashing, or some other means. But no, crucifixion was predicted and crucifixion it was.

His Resurrection

Psalm 16:10, also written by David, reads, ". . . because you will not abandon me to the grave, nor will you let your Holy One see decay." It is clear that David was prophesying about the Messiah. It could not be himself because he was not the *Holy One*, and his body after death did see decay. Furthermore, Jesus spoke about his death to come, to be followed by his resurrection.

There were many witnesses throughout the four gospels to his resurrection. Several women, including Mary Magdalene, saw the empty tomb, and were told by angels about Jesus exiting the tomb. There were a number of appearances in the presence of the disciples over a period of forty days according to Acts 1:3; and according to the Apostle Paul in 1 Corinthians 15:6, he appeared to a group of over 500 persons.

Comments by those who were not his followers are also of interest. There were writings in the decades following his death that attested to his resurrection. One of the most important was by Josephus, a Jew and a Pharisee, but not a Christian. In his book, *Antiquities of the Jews,* he made the following comment, also discussed in the previous chapter:

> Now there was about this time Jesus, a wise man, if it be lawful to call him a man, for he was a doer of wonderful works—a teacher of such men as receive the truth with pleasure. He drew over to him both many of the Jews, and many of the Gentiles. He was Christ; and when Pilate, at the suggestion of the principal men amongst us, had condemned him to the cross, those that loved him at the first did not forsake him, for he appeared to them alive again the third day, as the divine prophets had foretold these and ten thousand other wonderful things concerning him; the tribe of Christians, so named from him, are not extinct at this day.[4]

It is interesting to note the comment that "those that loved him at the first did not forsake him," As will be shown in chapter eight, the apostles and disciples fled in fear when Jesus was captured. After the resurrection, they were transformed to very bold men, carrying the message of the Gospel throughout the Middle East. All but one of the apostles were martyred for this cause.

A more modern testimonial to the reality of the resurrection came from Prof. Antony Flew, as discussed in chapter one. Flew, who for many decades was the foremost proponent of atheism, became a deist. In an article in the Baptist Press, Flew states he also believes Christians are intellectually justified in holding to their religion and that the resurrection of Jesus has more evidential support than any other reported miracle in history.[5] In a direct quote, he says, "The evidence for the resurrection is better than for claimed miracles in any other religion. It's outstandingly

---

4. Flavius Josephus, *Antiquities of the Jews*, xvii 3.3.

5. David Roach, *Famous Atheist Admits Evidence for God*, Baptist Press, reprinted in Christian Examiner, January 2005. Used with permission from the Baptist Press.

different in quality and quantity, I think, from the evidence offered for the occurrence of most other supposedly miraculous events."

The Amazing Isaiah 53

The fifty-third chapter of Isaiah is one of my favorite chapters in the Bible. It presents such a vivid prophecy of the Messiah, and fulfillment in Jesus Christ, that many critics were sure it had to be written after the time of Jesus. Until the discovery of the Dead Sea Scrolls, the oldest copy of Isaiah was from around 1000 AD. Among the Dead Sea Scrolls was a copy of Isaiah that predated Jesus by around 100 years, nullifying the criticisms. Isaiah 53:2–12 reads:

> He had no beauty or majesty to attract us to him, nothing in his appearance that we should desire him.
>
> He was despised and rejected of men, a man of sorrows, and familiar with suffering.
>
> Like one from whom men hide their faces he was despised, and we esteemed him not.
>
> Surely he took up our infirmities and carried our sorrows, yet we considered him stricken by God, smitten by him and afflicted.
>
> But he was pierced for our transgressions, he was crushed for our iniquities; the punishment that brought us peace was upon him, and by his wounds we are healed.
>
> We all, like sheep, have gone astray, each of us has turned to his own way; and the Lord has laid on him the iniquity of us all.
>
> He was oppressed and afflicted, yet he did not open his mouth; he was led like a lamb to the slaughter, and as a sheep before her shearers is silent, so he did not open his mouth.
>
> By oppression and judgment he was taken away. And who can speak of his descendants? For he was cut off from the land of the living; for the transgression of my people he was stricken.
>
> He was assigned a grave with the wicked, and with the rich in his death, though he had done no violence, nor was any deceit in his mouth.
>
> Yet it was the Lord's will to crush him and cause him to suffer, and though the Lord makes his life a guilt offering, he will see his offspring and prolong his days, and the will of the Lord will prosper in his hand.

After the suffering of his soul, he will see the light of life and be satisfied; by his knowledge my righteous servant will justify many, and he will bear their iniquities.

Therefore I will give him a portion among the great, and he will divide the spoils with the strong, because he poured out his life unto death, and was numbered among the transgressors.

For he bore the sins of many, and made intercession for the transgressors.

There are so many phrases in this chapter that describe what happened to Jesus and why. He was despised and rejected. He suffered. He was pierced. He was oppressed and afflicted. Why? Because of us—all of us. We are the transgressors—people of iniquities. We all have gone astray and turned into our own way. It was for our sins that he was afflicted and pierced. Even the prophecy about his grave was fulfilled. A rich man, Joseph of Arimathea, took Jesus' body and it was placed in the rich man's grave (Mark 15:43–46). Well, you get the idea. I could go on and on about the details that portray Jesus Christ in this chapter. As will be discussed in more detail in chapter seven, we are all sinners who need the covering of our sins for eternal life with a Holy God. Jesus provided that covering with his sacrifice on the cross.

In conclusion, how amazing are these prophecies salted and peppered throughout the Bible! Although I have not covered all of the messianic prophecies, I have selected a significant and representative body of such predictions—all of them fulfilled centuries later in Jesus Christ. How could there be a different Messiah, coming in the future, as some believe? No, too many prophecies have been fulfilled in Jesus. If a Messiah were to come in the future to die for our sins, who would crucify him? That form of execution has not been employed for a long time. No other person could match the numerous details called for in so many different locations in the Old and New Testaments.

RECOMMENDED READING

John F. Walvoord, Th.D., *The Prophecy Knowledge Handbook*, Wheaton: Victor Books, 1990.

D. James Kennedy, Ph.D., *Messiah: Prophecies Fulfilled,* Fort Lauderdale: Coral Ridge Ministries, 2003.

4

Types of Christ

The next day John saw Jesus coming toward him and said,
"Look, the Lamb of God, who takes away the sin of the world!"

John 1:29

WHAT ARE TYPES OF Christ, and why are they important? Types of Christ are individuals or other symbols that have parallels to characteristics of Jesus Christ. They are not exact replicas of Jesus, as no one could match his perfect life. However, there are sufficient parallels that they go beyond coincidence. Again, they are *salted and peppered* throughout the scriptures. Why are they important? I believe that, similar to prophecy, God has provided these metaphors in the Bible to give credence to Jesus Christ as Messiah and to provide evidence to support the believer's faith. As with prophecy, they occur throughout the Old and New Testaments.

Types are not peculiar to Jesus Christ alone. There are many other types in the Bible. In her book, *Study of the Types,*[1] Ada Habershon discusses many other forms of types. However for the purposes of this book, we will concentrate on just a few of the types of Christ. Our purpose here is to show that Jesus Christ as Messiah was foreshadowed in many ways throughout the Scriptures so there would be no mistaking that he was the one for whom God's people were waiting.

MOSES

In the book of Deuteronomy, the fifth book of the Old Testament, or the Hebrew Scriptures, Moses declares: "The Lord your God will raise up for

1. Ada R. Habershon, *Study of the Types*, Grand Rapids: Kregel Publications, 1974.

you a prophet *like me* (emphasis added) from among your own brothers" (Deuteronomy 18:15). Moses tells us about 1400 years before the birth of Christ that the Messiah will be "like me."

In what respect was Moses like Jesus? Habershon lists sixty-eight references to aspects of Moses' life that resembled the life of Jesus.[2] In Exodus, chapter three, we see Moses as a shepherd, tending the flock of his father-in-law Jethro. Moses had escaped from Egypt, where Pharaoh's daughter had raised him. He left his position of royalty after killing an Egyptian who was beating a Jew. In John 10:11, Jesus tells us, "I am the good shepherd. The good shepherd lays down his life for the sheep."

Moses was also a judge. Exodus 18:13 informs us, "The next day Moses took his seat to serve as judge for the people, and they stood around him from morning till evening." In the following passages, we learn that judging was one of Moses' major responsibilities. In the fifth chapter of the book of John, Jesus tells us the Father gave him the "authority to judge" (John 5:27, 30).

In many situations, Moses was also an intercessor for the people. He often went to the Lord to plead on their behalf. Jesus is the ultimate intercessor. In Romans 8:34 the apostle Paul tells us, "Christ Jesus, who died—more than that, who was raised to life—is at the right hand of God and is also interceding for us."

The apostle Luke informs us that Moses was a ruler, appointed by God, "He was sent to be their ruler and deliverer by God himself, through the angel who appeared to him in the bush. He led them out of Egypt and did wonders and miraculous signs in Egypt, at the Red Sea, and for forty years in the desert" (Acts 7:35–36). In the Old Testament book Micah, we have seen that the birthplace of the Christ was foretold to be Bethlehem. In the same passages, the Lord tells us the Messiah will be "ruler over Israel." Numerous New Testament passages speak of Jesus as the ultimate ruler over the entire universe. Moreover, just as the passage above speaks of Moses as a deliverer of his people, which we saw fulfilled in the exodus from Egypt, Jesus was the ultimate deliverer. In Romans 11:26–27, the apostle Paul quotes from Isaiah and Jeremiah in referring to Jesus, "The deliverer will come from Zion; he will turn godlessness away from Jacob. And this is my covenant with them when I take away their sins." Jesus

2. Ibid., 165–68.

came to earth to absolve us from our sins, and as such, is the ultimate deliverer.

I must emphasize here, although there were many similarities between Moses and Jesus, we must acknowledge that Jesus was unique in that he led a sinless life allowing him to be the sacrifice for our sins. Moses, while a great leader ordained by God and one who had similarities to Jesus in characteristics, he was not sinless. He committed murder, and one of his other sins prevented his entry to the Promised Land.

JOSEPH

Joseph is one of the most interesting characters in the Bible. Chapters 37 to 50 of the book of Genesis are primarily concerned with Joseph and his family. Why is that much space devoted to this topic? Is he in the lineage of David or Jesus Christ? No, he is not. His half-brother Judah is the ancestor of David and Jesus. I believe God chose Joseph to accomplish magnificent deeds because God foreknew Joseph's character, but also that he was to be a type of Christ.

Joseph's father Jacob was the grandson of the patriarch Abraham. Jacob was a victim of a swindle when he was betrothed to Rachel, his desired bride, whom he loved greatly. He agreed to work for his future father-in-law for seven years to receive Rachel as his wife. During the wedding, Laban substituted the older daughter Leah in place of Rachel. Jacob was devastated. Laban agreed to allow Jacob to wed Rachel if he would work for another seven years, which he did.

Leah began to bear Jacob sons. Four sons were born to her, while Rachel was apparently barren. Envious of Leah, Rachel gave her maid Bilhah to Jacob as another wife, and Bilhah bore two sons. The competition continued when Leah gave Jacob her maid also. Her maid Zilpah bore two sons, followed by two more sons from Leah. Finally, Rachel had a son, Joseph.

Because Joseph was the son of Jacob's first love, he showed the boy a great deal of favoritism. Many persons, who have attended Sunday school classes as children, learned the story of Joseph and the multicolored robe Jacob made for him. Jacob was a flawed individual, and his favoritism had extremely negative consequences. Joseph complicated the circumstances further by telling his half-brothers he had dreams in which he would have dominance over them.

When Joseph was sent into the fields where his half-brothers were tending the flocks, they plotted to kill him. One of his brothers, Reuben, dissuaded them from killing him, but they threw him in a cistern, and later sold him to a caravan of traders. They took his robe, dipped it in goat's blood and took it back to his father. Jacob concluded Joseph had been killed, and he was devastated.

Joseph was sold to Potiphar, one of Pharaoh's officials. The Bible tells us the Lord was with Joseph, and he prospered. Potiphar placed Joseph in charge of his household. Unfortunately, Potiphar's wife lusted after Joseph. When Joseph resisted her advances, she accused Joseph of attacking her. Potiphar believed her and had Joseph imprisoned.

Some time later, the Pharaoh became angry with two of his servants and had them placed under confinement. One night, each of them had dreams, which Joseph interpreted. His interpretations came true. Two years later, Pharaoh had two dreams. but no one was able to interpret them. It was brought to Pharaoh's attention that a prisoner had the capability to make the interpretations. When Joseph was brought to Pharaoh, he stated that he could not make interpretations, but God would give the answers.

Joseph explained to Pharaoh both dreams meant the same thing. God had revealed there would be seven years of great abundance, then seven years of famine. Joseph gave Pharaoh a plan of saving food during the years of plenty so there would be food in the years of famine. As a result, Pharaoh gave Joseph dominion over the whole land of Egypt to execute the plan Joseph had generated. After the years of plenty, people came from far off countries to buy food in Egypt.

When Jacob's family was desperate for food, he sent all but his youngest son Benjamin to Egypt to buy food. When they arrived in Egypt, they were brought before Joseph, who recognized them, although they did not recognize him. Joseph could have exacted vengeance upon them, but he did not. He did give them a bit of a hard time, but he sent them back home with grain and had returned their silver in their sacks. He also ordered them to bring Benjamin on the next trip.

When they returned to buy more grain, they brought Benjamin with them, and Joseph again played some tricks on them. Finally, he made himself known to them, and they were terrified, but he comforted them and told them not to be afraid. He sent them back to bring Jacob and the remaining family members to Egypt. He then made arrangements with Pharaoh for them to have land and to prosper.

After Jacob's death, the brothers again were fearful that Joseph might exact vengeance upon them, but Joseph told them, "Don't be afraid. Am I in the place of God? You intended to harm me, but God intended it for good to accomplish what is now being done, the saving of many lives. So then, don't be afraid. I will provide for you and your children" (Genesis 50:19–21).

Genesis 46:27 informs us, "With the two sons that had been born to Joseph in Egypt, the members of Jacob's family, which went to Egypt, were seventy in all. Exodus 1:6–7 states, "Now Joseph and all his brothers and all that generation died, but the Israelites were fruitful and multiplied greatly and became exceedingly numerous, so that the land was filled with them." This is a key comment. Joseph's brothers and his two sons became the twelve tribes of Israel. When they left Egypt during the exodus, their numbers were huge.

So let's consider some possibilities. What if his brothers killed Joseph as a callow youth? What if he was not imprisoned by Potiphar, and his ability to interpret dreams did not become apparent to Pharaoh? What if Pharaoh did not have dreams that needed to be interpreted? There are a number of what-ifs that could have changed the course of history. The key here again is Joseph's quotation above. God arranged the circumstances that led to Joseph's ascension to the position of second in command in Egypt to save God's chosen people. Could God have accomplished these ends another way if some of the what-ifs had come to pass? Of course he could. However, the story of Joseph is rife with God accomplishing his plan.

Now let us consider some aspects of Joseph's life that foreshadowed Jesus Christ. Habershon lists over 100 factors of similarity between Joseph and Jesus.[3] As with Moses' story above, Joseph was a shepherd. When we first encounter him in Genesis 37, he is tending the flocks with his brothers. As also stated above, Jesus referred to himself as the good shepherd. In Genesis 37:3, we learn how much Joseph is loved by his father, and Matthew 3:17 relates God's words about Jesus: "And a voice from heaven said, 'This is my Son, whom I love; with him I am well pleased.'"

As much as Jesus and Joseph were loved by their fathers, others also hated them. I have already related how Joseph's brothers hated him. Jesus, who did so much to teach people about love, healed the infirm, etc., was also hated by many, especially the religious and political leaders of His day. In John 15:23–25, Jesus tells us of one of many hateful circumstances:

---

3. Ibid., 169–74.

"He who hates me hates my Father as well. If I had not done among them what no one else did, they would not be guilty of sin. But now they have seen these miracles, and yet they have hated both me and my Father. But this is to fulfill what is written in their Law: 'They hated me without reason.'" The latter is a comment from Psalm 69.

Both Joseph and Jesus were conspired against by those who hated them, both were stripped of their clothing, and both were imprisoned unjustly. His brothers sold Joseph to the Ishmaelites for twenty shekels of silver. Judas betrayed Jesus for thirty silver coins. However, all of their travails resulted in the saving of lives. In the case of Joseph, it was his family, which then emerged as the nation of Israel. With Jesus, his sacrifice saves for all eternity every one who believes in Him.

ESTHER

The book of Esther is a fascinating story about one of the types of Christ, and it is also an old-fashioned melodrama. The villain is a man named Haman. In the old melodramas, the oppressed one was a fair-haired maiden. Here the oppressed ones are Mordecai and the Jewish nation. The hero, or in this case heroine, is Esther.

Early in the book, we learn she is an orphan, adopted and raised by her cousin, Mordecai. Nebuchadnezzar had carried Mordecai's family into exile from Jerusalem. Esther was like a daughter to Mordecai. Later, during Persian rule, King Xerxes threw ostentatious parties in the capital city of Susa. Military leaders, princes, and other nobles attended the parties. There was considerable drinking involved, and at a point when Xerxes was "in high spirits from wine," he summoned Queen Vashti to come to his banquet so all could see her beauty. The queen refused to appear, and after some bad advice from his cronies, Xerxes deposed Vashti as queen.

After a period of time, Xerxes decided to find a new queen. A search of the entire realm was made, and many beautiful women were brought into the harem. Esther was one of these beautiful women who was selected. Over a long period of time, each woman spent the night with the king. Amazingly, out of so many beautiful women, Esther was the one the king chose to be his new queen. Could this be a divine appointment? Let's continue and see how the melodrama unfolds.

At this point in the story, Mordecai plays an important role. He overhears a plot to kill the king, and he relates the scheme to Esther. She in turn tells the story to the king and gives credit to Mordecai. The conspirators are executed, and the circumstances are recorded in the Persian book of chronicles.

Meanwhile, Haman was elevated to a position just under the king. Wherever he goes, people are required to bow before him. Even noblemen kneel in his presence. All that is except Mordecai, who refuses to do so, thereby inciting Haman's wrath. Haman plots to kill not only Mordecai, but also all Jews throughout the realm. He convinces the king that these people are evil and should be annihilated. The king decides to approve Haman's plot. Once again God's people are threatened with extinction. If they are eradicated, from where will the prophesied Messiah arise?

Mordecai gets a message to Esther about Haman's treachery, and he suggests she go to the king to plead for her people. Initially, she refuses, because she is fearful for her life. Even a queen cannot go before the king without being summoned. Execution may result. Mordecai sends her another message ending in the memorable words: "And who knows but that you have come to royal position for such a time as this?" (Esther 4:14). What an idea! Was divine providence involved in Esther being selected from a large number of beautiful women because God knew she would be in a position to save his chosen people?

Esther relents. She asks Mordecai to get all the Jews in Susa to join her in a fast for three days. She then utters her own memorable and courageous words: "When this is done, I will go to the king, even though it is against the law. And if I perish, I perish" (Esther 4:16). What courage! She then goes to the king, who fortunately welcomes her. She requests that he and Haman attend two successive banquets she will provide.

Meanwhile, Haman hatches another plot, this time to hang Mordecai on a gallows. Here another amazing "coincidence" occurs. The king cannot sleep. He decides, as many persons do in a similar situation, to read something to help him sleep. Here's where it gets interesting. He decides to read the book of the chronicles of his reign. We do not know how he goes about his selection process, but he picks the exact place in the chronicles, which describes how Mordecai saved his life. Is this another God-directed activity?

He asks his attendants what has been done for Mordecai, and they respond that nothing has been done. At this point, Haman shows up to talk to the king about hanging Mordecai—talk about a great sense of timing! Before Haman makes his request, the king asks him what should be done for one whom the king wishes to honor. Of course, Haman thinks the king means him. So he suggests the man be royally clothed and led on a horse through the city streets. The king tells Haman to honor Mordecai as Haman has described. Haman is mortified! Who says the Bible does not contain humor!

After the parade through the city, Haman is escorted to Esther's banquet. The king asks Esther what is the request she has for him. She asks the king to save her and her people from the edict Haman brought about, which would lead to her death and the death of the Israelites. As a result, Haman is hanged on his own gallows, and the Jews are saved from annihilation. Of course, I have condensed the story, but it is a wonderful read, and I include it in my recommended reading list at the end of the chapter.

Let's now consider the factors that make Esther a type of Christ. First, she was willing to give up her life: "If I perish, I perish." Of course, unlike Jesus, she was not executed, but she was willing. Secondly, she saved her people. Without her courageous intrusion before the king, the Jews would have been exterminated.

The melodrama is filled with fascinating ironies. Haman, who thinks he will be honored, is forced to honor the man he hates the most. He is hanged on a gallows that he built for Mordecai. Esther, who could have been executed, is welcomed by the king. The sleepless king reads a key passage in his chronicles at a very timely point. God's chosen people could have been eliminated; instead, they are allowed to defend themselves, and in the process eliminate many enemies. Most importantly, the people from whom the Savior will arise are preserved.

BOAZ

Boaz is one of the principal characters in the Book of Ruth, the eighth book of the Old Testament. Whereas Esther was a melodrama, Ruth is a miniature romance novel, crammed into four brief chapters. The story begins with a man named Elimelech, who takes his wife Naomi and two sons to Moab because of a famine in his homeland. Elimelech dies in Moab. His sons take two Moabite women as their wives, one of whom was Ruth. After ten years, both of Naomi's sons also die.

Naomi prepares to return to Judah, where the famine was over. She tells her two daughters-in-law to go back to their mother's home in Moab, and one of them tearfully leaves. In spite of Naomi's urging, Ruth stays with her, uttering one of the most beautiful passages in the Bible:

> Don't urge me to leave you or to turn back from you. Where you go I will go, and where you stay I will stay. Your people will be my people and your God my God. Where you die I will die, and there I will be buried. May the Lord deal with me, be it ever so severely, if anything but death separates you and me. Ruth (1:16–17).

So, they move to Judah with no resources on which to live. Boaz is a relative of Naomi's, so she tells Ruth to go and glean grain in his fields. When Boaz sees her, he inquires as to who she is. He then goes to Ruth and tells her to glean only in his fields, and she will be protected from any harm. He gives her water and tells the harvesters to leave behind extra grain for her to pick up.

Realizing that Boaz is a "kinsman-redeemer," Naomi tells Ruth how to approach him so he might offer to marry her. After clearing the situation with another "kinsman-redeemer" who is a closer relative of Naomi's, Boaz marries Ruth. Ruth bears Boaz a son, and his lineage will continue—a very important fact.

This is a lovely romance story. Out of tragedy for Naomi and Ruth comes a whole new direction for their lives with love, provisions for their needs, and security. But what is this story doing in the Bible? For one thing, Boaz is a type of Christ. By redeeming Ruth, he saves her life and Naomi's from poverty, hunger, and possibly death.

However, there is even more to this story. Their son is named Obed, and he is the father of Jesse, who is the father of David. As we know, David is the ancestor of Jesus. Here, centuries before the birth of Jesus, is placed a historical book about two of the ancestors of the Messiah. This is why continuation of Boaz's lineage is so important. Boaz lives in Bethlehem, the future birthplace of Jesus, the "Son of David" and the Messiah.

Now let us fast-forward to the first chapter of the book of Matthew, the first book of the New Testament, where we find the genealogy of Jesus. In verse five, we read, "Boaz the father of Obed, whose mother was Ruth." In those days it was very unusual to have women's names appear in genealogies. In forty-two named generations, starting all the way back to Abraham, only four women are named. One of them is Ruth, and another is Mary, Jesus' mother.

Now we can see why this little book is so important. Boaz is a type of Christ, and he is an ancestor of Christ. The author of the book knew the importance of this wonderful romance, pointing to the coming of Jesus, the Messiah. Through the inspiration of the Holy Spirit, it was written and assumed its rightful and important place in the Jewish Scriptures, the Old Testament, centuries before the birth of Jesus.

LAMB OF GOD

There are two aspects of a lamb in the Bible that bring to mind the concept of a type of Christ. First, lambs are mentioned throughout the first five books of the Bible, or the books of the Law, as animals sacrificed for atonement, or forgiveness of sins (Leviticus 4:32–35). The absolution of sins provided the restoration of the relationship with the Holy God. Another reference to a lamb pertinent to this issue is the Passover lamb. In the book of Exodus, God directed Moses to go to Pharaoh to free the Israelites from their slavery in Egypt. Pharaoh refused, and God brought nine plagues upon the nation. After each plague, Moses pleaded with Pharaoh to let the people go. When Pharaoh resolutely refused for the ninth time, God decided the only way to change Pharaoh's mind and free the Israelites was by the death of the Egyptian firstborn children. The Israelites were instructed to place the blood of a lamb on the top and sides of the doorway. By this sign, the angel would "pass over" the household, and the occupants would be saved. The Egyptians, who did not have the protection of the blood of the lamb, were slain, and Pharaoh relented.

The lamb is a type of Christ, because in his sacrifice on the cross, the blood of Jesus saved all who would believe in him and his atonement for their sin. In the Isaiah 53 prophecy about the Messiah, we read, "He was led like a lamb to the slaughter" (Isaiah 53:7). In the New Testament, there are many references to Jesus as a lamb. When John the Baptist was preaching and baptizing people in the area near Bethany, he sees Jesus approaching and declares, "Look, the Lamb of God, who takes away the sin of the world!" (John 1:29). The next day, he sees Jesus again and says, "Look, the Lamb of God" (John 1:36).

In the book of Acts, written by the apostle and doctor Luke, Philip is directed to talk to an Ethiopian eunuch who had traveled to Jerusalem to worship and was returning to his home. He was reading from Isaiah 53, including the passage about the lamb before its shearer. He asked Philip to explain the meaning of the words in the chapter. Philip "told him about the good news about Jesus." The Ethiopian asked to be baptized in some nearby water and Philip did so.

Then in 1 Peter 1:18–19, Peter tells us, "For you know that it was not with perishable things such as silver and gold that you were redeemed from the empty way of life handed down to you from your forefathers, but with the precious blood of Christ, a lamb without blemish or defect."

The book of Revelation is the last book in the Bible. It was written by the apostle John, who also wrote the Gospel of John. In the book, there are twenty-nine references to the lamb, which are glorifications of Jesus Christ. In Revelation 5:12, we read, "Worthy is the Lamb, who was slain, to receive power and wealth and wisdom and strength and honor and glory and praise!" Further, in verse thirteen, "To him who sits on the throne and to the Lamb be praise and honor and glory and power, for ever and ever!" The identification of Jesus as the Lamb of God is carried throughout the book. It is clear the lamb is another type of Christ.

SHEPHERDS

I have partially covered shepherds as types of Christ in sections above. However, there is more to be said about this unusual category of laborer. Let's consider some of the characteristics of shepherds and see how they might apply to Jesus Christ. Then I will show some events from the Bible as corroboration of this concept.

First, let's think of the characteristics of shepherds. They must be trustworthy, for they tend a very valuable commodity. They care for the sheep. They see that the sheep are fed. When one wanders, they bring the errant one back into the fold. They protect them from predators. In fact, they will risk their lives for the safety of their flock. We may think of shepherds as pretty ordinary people, but the teachings of the Bible show otherwise. Some great men of the Bible were shepherds. We have mentioned Moses and Joseph, who spent periods of time as shepherds. Jacob, Joseph's father, also labored as a shepherd, working for fourteen years for his father-in-law so he could receive the woman he loved. And the great King David, who slew Goliath and led great campaigns against the Philistines and other enemies of Israel, started life as a shepherd. Although the Persian king, Cyrus, was not a literal shepherd, the Lord says of him, "He is my shepherd and will accomplish all that I please; he will say of Jerusalem, 'Let it be rebuilt'" (Isaiah 44:28). Moreover, one of the greatest psalms of David, Psalm 23, speaks of the Lord as a shepherd: "The Lord is my Shepherd, I shall not be in want. He makes me lie down in green pastures, he leads me beside quiet waters, he restores my soul."

When Jesus wants to illustrate how important every individual soul is to the Father, he uses a parable about sheep: "If a man owns a hundred sheep, and one of them wanders away, will he not leave the ninety-nine on the hills and go to look for the one that wandered off? And if he finds it, I tell you the truth, he is happier about that one sheep than about the ninety-nine that did not wander off. In the same way your Father in heaven is not willing that any of these little ones should be lost" (Matthew 18:12–14).

Another important passage occurs after Jesus' resurrection when he appears to the disciples by the Sea of Tiberias. The disciples at this point have gone back to their trade as fishermen. Jesus singles out Peter for an important conversation. Peter had denied Jesus three times as predicted by Jesus, but Jesus still had great plans for this potential leader. He asks Peter three times if Peter loves him. After each question, Peter answers in the affirmative that he loves Jesus. After the first reply, Jesus tells him, "Feed my lambs." After the second reply, Jesus says, "Take care of my sheep." And again upon the third reply, he says, "Feed my sheep." Jesus is not talking about physical feeding. Jesus is preparing Peter to be a great spiritual leader of the church. The feeding is about spiritual food the early church members will need to face the great challenges that will be before them.

Before I leave the subject of shepherds, there is another Biblical passage illustrating that shepherds even transcended royalty. In the second chapter of Luke in the New Testament, we are told the story of the birth of Jesus. When the birth was at hand, who was invited to the birthday party? It was not the failed spiritual leaders of Israel, the Pharisees, Sadducees, or High Priest. It was not the political leadership of the day, the Sanhedrin or King Herod. Fortunately, the latter was not invited; after all, he tried to kill the baby Jesus. Let's read the passage to see who were invited to the party:

> And there were shepherds living out in the fields nearby, keeping watch over their flocks at night. An angel of the Lord appeared to them, and the glory of the Lord shone around them, and they were terrified. But the angel said to them, 'Do not be afraid. I bring you good news of great joy that will be for all the people. Today in the town of David a Savior has been born to you; he is Christ the Lord. This will be a sign to you: You will find a baby wrapped in cloths

and lying in a manger.' Suddenly a great company of the heavenly host appeared with the angel, praising God and saying, 'Glory to God in the highest, and on earth peace to men on whom his favor rests.' When the angels had left them and gone into heaven, the shepherds said to one another, 'Let's go to Bethlehem and see this thing that has happened, which the Lord has told us about.' So they hurried off and found Mary and Joseph, and the baby, who was lying in the manger. When they had seen him, they spread the word concerning what had been told them about this child, and all who heard it were amazed at what the shepherds said to them. But Mary treasured up all these things and pondered them in her heart. The shepherds returned, glorifying and praising God for all the things they had heard and seen, which were just as they had been told. (Luke 2:8–20).

Isn't it fascinating that not only were shepherds a specially invited group to witness the newly born Jesus, but they were also the messengers chosen to go out among the people to spread the word about this great event the people had been looking forward to for many centuries: In the town of Bethlehem, their Messiah, the Savior Jesus Christ, had been born. Like Jesus, the shepherds were bearers of good news.

RECOMMENDED READING

Ada R. Habershon, *Study of the Types*, Grand Rapids: Kregel Publications, 1974.

Exodus, Chapters 1–20; 32–34.

Numbers, Chapter 20.

Deuteronomy, Chapters 31–34.

Genesis, Chapters 37–50.

Book of Esther.

Book of Ruth.

5

God's Ways are Different than Man's Ways

For my thoughts are not your thoughts, neither are your ways my ways,
declares the Lord. As the heavens are higher than the earth, so are my ways
higher than your ways and my thoughts than your thoughts.

Isaiah 55:8-9

There is a way that seems right to a man, but in the end it leads to death.

Proverbs 14:12

In Philip Yancey's book, *What's so Amazing About Grace,*[1] he discusses a conference during which experts from around the world debated what was unique to the Christian faith. Eventually, C.S. Lewis wandered in. When he found out the subject of the discussion, he responded, "Oh, that's easy. It's grace." Yancey goes on to say: "The notion of God's love coming to us free of charge, no strings attached, seems to go against every instinct of humanity." Man's way is to *earn* acceptance by God. In other religions, one has to earn acceptance by God. God's way is unique in that salvation is not earned, and the uniqueness of God's way is affirming to my faith.

In discussing belief systems with non-Christian friends and acquaintances who believe in a supreme being, I have heard over and over again the idea that as long as one's good behavior outweighs the bad, one can expect to be accepted into God's heaven. Moreover, some persons have a tendency to set up criteria for what God should be like for them to believe in him. This concept has been termed, "creating God in man's image." Man says, "This is how I want it to be, therefore it is so." How often have you

1. Philip Yancey, *What's So Amazing About Grace?* Grand Rapids: Zondervan, 1997, 45.

heard someone say they cannot believe in God because he allows evil in the world, or bad things happen to good people, and so forth. Such conclusions are unfortunate, because of the many dear people who hold to such theories. God's way is different and incredibly better for mankind, as we shall see in chapter seven.

Why are God's ways different? Why cannot they be as mankind might wish? One reason is that God is omniscient. He sees the beginning from the end. God's omniscience means that something we may believe is negative is serving some higher purpose we know nothing about. For example, one with limited knowledge of the purpose behind Jesus' cru-cifixion might conclude: "That is a terrible thing to happen." Yes, Jesus suffered horribly, but it resulted in a way for human beings to be forgiven for their sins and experience eternal life with God.

Why does it make a difference that God's ways are different than man's ways? The reason is, if all of God's principles and actions were exactly as an intelligent human would produce, what would be unique about God? He would be reduced to a superior human being. However, if we can show that God's ways are indeed unique and different than an intelligent man would produce, we gain insight to how God his omniscient, all-powerful, and far above mankind. It is evidence for is existence, sovereignty, creativity, and worthiness to be esteemed and trusted as our creator. To illustrate the uniqueness of God's ways, I have selected a number of illustrative situations in the Bible. Choice of leaders, God's use of godless men, and the veneration of women are some of the topics covered in this chapter.

CHOICE OF LEADERS

How does man select his leaders? Typically, in most walks of life, we run competitions. In industry, someone from a group stands out because of hard work, intelligence, experience, and many other factors. A promotion is granted on the basis of such factors. Sometimes other parameters, such as favoritism, enter into the equation. Based on such judgments, someone is elevated to the next level of supervision. As for our political leaders, there are similar procedures at work. However, there are many additional determinants. For high-level positions, such as president, there is a great deal of media attention. We have debates, television interviews, "barn-storming" throughout the nation, and speeches in various assembled meetings. And we have many pundits telling us who won the debates, and who has the best grasp of issues, and so forth. Is it any wonder that we have so many leaders who are disappointing? I once reported to a manager who was hired on the basis of a single interview with an executive vice-president because he was good at selling himself. He was later fired, after a lot of damage was done.

God chose many leaders who would not be the first choice of even a very intelligent evaluator. Let us take a look at some of these situations. In chapter eight, I will cover in more detail the amazing transformation of the apostle Paul, formerly known as Saul. He was a Pharisee and a very intelligent man who had been trained by the eminent scholar and Pharisee, Gamaliel. Unfortunately, Saul took it upon himself to find followers of Jesus Christ and have them imprisoned. He also was present at the stoning of the innocent man, Stephen (Acts 7). He was truly a feared enemy of the Christian church. Who would choose this man to become an apostle and great leader in the church? God did. On a trip to Damascus, Jesus intervened in the life of Saul. He was miraculously transformed and was responsible for many thousands of conversions to Christianity during his life, and his New Testament writings have influenced millions to follow Jesus Christ.

Another apostle, Peter, was a coward. He denied knowing Jesus three times, after Jesus was taken prisoner prior to his crucifixion. After Jesus' death, Peter was in hiding with the other apostles, fearing for his life. Again, he would not appear to be one whom we would select to follow in furthering the church of Christ. However, he spent time with the resurrected Jesus, who asked Peter to "feed my sheep." He was transformed into a fearless man who defied the authorities by preaching in public. He even was imprisoned and lashed, but he became one of the truly great leaders of the early church and also wrote books of the New Testament.

Another very unlikely choice for a leader was a man named Gideon (Judges 6–8). At the time, the Midianites and other surrounding peoples oppressed the Israelites. God heard the cries of his people and decided to rescue them. Whom did he choose to lead them? Gideon, who was threshing wheat at the time; not exactly the job description for a warrior. When God told Gideon to go and save Israel, did Gideon respond enthusiastically as would be expected from an army general in the making? Here are his words, "But Lord, how can I save Israel? My clan is the weakest in Manasseh, and I am the least in my family" (Judges 6:15). God tells Gideon that he will be with him and he will be successful. After Gideon asks for, and receives, a sign from God, he agrees to go forward and serve the Lord. But God does not make it easy for him.

Thirty-two thousand men are gathered to fight the Midianites, but God declares that there are too many men. In a series of tests, he reduces the number to three hundred! The Lord's instructions involve the three hundred men using clay jars, torches, and trumpets. When God gave the signal, the men broke the jars, exposing the torches. They also blew the trumpets. There was incredible confusion among the Midianites, and God caused them to turn on each other. As the Midianites fled, they were also set upon by other Israelite tribes, and the Midianites were crushed. God used a wheat-thresher to lead a miniscule band to victory over thousands of enemy soldiers.

There are many other stories in the Bible of God using people that would not be thought of as leaders. Moses was a murderer and had a speech impediment, but God chose him to lead the Israelites out of Egypt. David was the least of seven brothers. When the prophet and judge, Samuel, came to anoint the new king of Israel, God rejected in turn all of the older brothers, stating, "The Lord does not look at the things man looks at. Man looks at the outward appearance, but the Lord looks at the heart" (1 Samuel 16:7). There we have the clue to God's selection process. Where is David when all this is taking place? He is not even present. He is tending the sheep. He is then brought in, and at God's direction, Samuel anoints David king.

I can continue to name many other similar persons in the Bible. In all these cases of leaders and many others throughout the Scriptures, we see flawed, often very weak men chosen by God to accomplish incredible tasks. They are not the kind of people that would be obvious choices to be successful leaders as in the case of David. Why did God choose them? While we do not know for sure, there are some conclusions that are likely. The fact that they were very successful indicates that God saw in them characteristics he could shape to bring his plans to fruition. As stated, God knows the person's heart. Secondly, because they were flawed, it was clear that their accomplishments were because the power of God went before them. We see these situations in modern times also. God is still using imperfect men and women to bring about his purposes and further the growth of his church. We recognize God can accomplish the impossible if we have faith in him.

GOD'S USE OF GODLESS MEN

God also used godless men to bring about his plans and purposes. Personally, I and many other believers in God would not do things this way. But I am a man, and I think like a man. When one examines how God used these nonbelievers, it again shows that God is sovereign. It does not matter whom he chooses, a flawed believing leader, or a godless person who will bring about God's desired results. He will bring about his plans. One of the reasons God used such persons was to punish Israel when they disrespected God. The Scriptures show that he was always patient, and he sent many messages through his prophets to bring his chosen people back to him, but the messages were frequently ignored. Worse, the prophets were often harmed after delivering God's messages. The results often were the Israelites being conquered by other peoples in contrast with their many victories when they were obedient.

One of the great stories is about Nebuchadnezzar, the Babylonian king, who conquered Israel and brought the bulk of the Israelites to Babylonia, thereby fulfilling prophesies by Jeremiah and Ezekiel. The book of Daniel tells us much about Nebuchadnezzar's reign and contains wonderful prophecies, some of which were covered in chapter three. Daniel was one of the conscripted Israelites who rose to power under Nebuchadnezzar because the king had dreams his wise men could not interpret. In fact, the king required the wise men not only to interpret the dream, but also to tell him what was in the dream without him telling them. Of course, they were unable to do this. However, Daniel made it known that God would provide what the king desired. He prayed to God and the meaning of the dream was made known to him. As a result, the king made Daniel ruler over Babylon. This is what this pagan king had to say about Daniel's God: "Surely your God is the God of gods and the Lord of kings and a revealer of mysteries, for you were able to reveal this mystery" (Daniel 2:47).

Later, because of his pride, Nebuchadnezzar fell out of favor with God and was punished for a time. Was he resentful and bitter toward God? No. He knew he was experiencing something supernatural, and he was humbled. At the end of his time of punishment, these were his words:

> At the end of that time, I, Nebuchadnezzar, raised my eyes toward
> heaven, and my sanity was restored. Then I praised the Most High;
> I honored and glorified him who lives forever. His dominion is

an eternal dominion; his kingdom endures from generation to generation. All the peoples of the earth are regarded as nothing. He does as he pleases with the powers of heaven and the peoples of the earth. No one can hold back his hand or say to him: "What have you done?" (Daniel 4:34–35).

Cyrus was the king of Persia who conquered the Babylonians. The book of Ezra records how God used this pagan king: "In the first year of Cyrus king of Persia, in order *to fulfill the word of the Lord spoken by Jeremiah, the Lord moved the heart of Cyrus the king of Persia* to make a proclamation throughout his realm and to put it in writing" (Ezra 1:1) (emphasis added). What follows next are Cyrus' own words showing that God had directed his actions: "The Lord, the God of heaven, has given me all the kingdoms of the earth and he has appointed me to build a temple for him at Jerusalem in Judah" (Ezra 1:2). Cyrus then issued a proclamation that the exiles could go back to Jerusalem to rebuild the temple. He also provided gold, silver, and livestock to accomplish the task; and he returned the articles from the temple Nebuchadnezzar had removed to Babylon. What king would give up such treasures willingly if the sovereign God had not influenced him?

Similarly, God used King Artaxerxes to allow the king's cupbearer, Nehemiah, to take a cadre of individuals to rebuild the walls of Jerusalem. We also saw in chapter four how King Xerxes saved the nation of Israel through Esther's risking execution to make her plea for her people. Moreover, in chapter three, we described how Caesar Augustus issued a timely proclamation that took Mary and Joseph back to Bethlehem where Jesus was born in accordance with the prophecy of Micah. These are but a few examples of God's sovereignty in his relationships with his creation. He may employ weak or flawed men or women to fulfill his purposes, or he may influence great kings to bring about events that further his plans.

VENERATION OF WOMEN

Women in the cultures over the centuries spanned by the Bible were not highly regarded. In fact, they were little more than chattel. Women, in most cases, were legally owned by their fathers. When they married, the ownership passed on to their husbands. If a husband died, he could have willed his property to his wife, but she could not sell it. She would pass it on to a son. Daughters were not eligible. Women could be sold as slaves.

Moreover, it was unusual for women to be mentioned in any documents. Deirdre Good, professor of New Testament studies at General Theological Seminary, was quoted as saying: "The amazing thing is that there are any women at all in the ancient texts."[2] It was not just true of the Israelites, but of the surrounding nations as well. It was man's way.

In contrast, God's way toward women in the Bible is different. Many women are named in the Bible. In a listing contained in *Women of the Bible,*[3] I counted 57 women who are named. In addition, I counted 41 individuals or groups of women who were not named, but were designated by descriptions. Women had a wide variety of roles in the Scriptures. Two books of the Old Testament were named for women, Ruth and Esther, as previously discussed. In the beginning of the book of Matthew, the genealogy of Jesus Christ contains the names of four women, including Ruth and Mary. In contrast, secular genealogies never contained the names of women.

Deborah was a judge who led the Israelite army to victory over the Canaanites. Some women such as Huldah, Miriam, and Philip's daughter were prophetesses. Many were numbered among the disciples. Some, such as Phoebe, Priscilla, and others were leaders or hosts of house churches. There were various queens mentioned: Esther, Vashti, and the Queen of Sheba. There also were many women who were heroines at great risk to their lives. Rahab was a prostitute who put her life on the line when she aided two of Joshua's spies to escape entrapment. She later was married and became Boaz's mother, Jesus' ancestor, and one of the few women mentioned in Matthew's genealogy (Matthew 1:5). Pharaoh's daughter raised Moses as her own son at a time when her father decreed that Hebrew male children be killed. Jael and Jehosheba also risked their lives in heroic activity.

Another woman who had an important role included Mary Magdalene, who was healed by Jesus and became an important financial supporter. She was present when Jesus was crucified and at his burial. While the disciples had fled and were in hiding, Mary went to the grave and was the first to see he was no longer there. She was the first to speak to Jesus after his resurrection and brought the news to the disciples.

Jesus, who displayed the ultimate love for mankind by his sacrifice on the cross, also displayed his love in many other ways in the Scriptures.

2. Deirdre Goode, *Newsweek*, December 8, 2003, 59.

3. Sue P. Richards and Lawrence O. Richards, *Women of the Bible*, Nashville: Thomas Nelson, 2003.

He treated women and children with great kindness. In John 8, some religious leaders brought to Jesus a woman who had been caught in adultery. They were always trying to trap him. In the presence of a group of people, they stated that the law called for her to be stoned and asked him what to do. He did not respond immediately, but when they persisted, he said, "If any one of you is without sin, let him be the first to throw a stone at her" (John 8:7). The men all left, and Jesus told the woman to go and leave her life of sin. In another situation, women were bringing little children to him. When the disciples saw this, they rebuked the women. But Jesus said, "Let the little children come to me, and do not hinder them, for the kingdom of God belongs to such as these" (Luke 18:16).

Finally, there is the story of Mary, Jesus' mother and the most important woman in the Bible. Mary was a virgin and it is believed she was a teenager when she was visited by an angel who declared, "Greetings, you who are highly favored! The Lord is with you" (Luke 1:28). The Bible tells us she was greatly troubled by his words; then the angel tells her, "Do not be afraid, Mary, you have found favor with God. You will be with child and give birth to a son, and you are to give him the name Jesus. He will be great and will be called the Son of the Most High. The Lord will give him the throne of his father David, and he will reign over the house of Jacob forever; his kingdom will never end" (Luke 1:30–33). (Author's note: It was common to refer to an ancestor such as David here with the term, "father.") The angel went on to explain that there would not be an earthly father of the child, but that the Holy Spirit would accomplish the conception.

At this point, Mary could have been fearful and very negative. After all, she was a virgin at the time. She was betrothed to Joseph, and he might think she had an affair, with possibly deadly consequences. However, Mary had faith in her Lord. She responded, "I am the Lord's servant. May it be to me as you have said" (Luke 1:38). Fortunately, an angel also visited Joseph and explained the situation to him as well (Matthew 1:20–23).

The veneration and love shown to her by God inspired Mary to express her gratitude to the Lord as follows:

> My soul glorifies the Lord and my spirit rejoices in God my Savior, for he has been mindful of the humble state of his servant. From now on all generations will call me blessed, for the Mighty One has done great things for me—holy is his name. His mercy extends to those who fear him, from generation to generation. He has performed mighty deeds with his arm; he has scattered those who are

proud in their inmost thoughts. He has brought down rulers from their thrones but has lifted up the humble. He has filled the hungry with good things but has sent the rich away empty. He has helped his servant Israel, remembering to be merciful to Abraham and his descendants forever, even as he said to our fathers (Luke 1:46–55).

RECOMMENDED READING

Sue P. Richards and Lawrence O. Richards, *Women of the Bible*, Nashville: Thomas Nelson, 2003.

6

Consistency between the Old and New Testaments

All Scripture is God-breathed and is useful for teaching, rebuking, correcting and training in righteousness, so that the man of God may be thoroughly equipped for every good work.

2 Timothy 3:16

EVIDENCE FOR THE AUTHORITY of the Bible would require consistency throughout. As stated by Augustine more than 1,500 years ago, "The New is in the Old Testament contained; the Old is in the New explained." God is a consistent God. If he inspired all the books of the Bible, shouldn't we expect there to be a consistent pattern from beginning to end? In spite of sixty-six books by over forty authors, we see a remarkable consistency throughout.

While the Old Testament is written mostly in Hebrew and the New Testament is written mostly in Greek, they are both Jewish books. With the probable exception of Luke, all of the New Testament writers were Jews, as were the authors of the Old Testament Scriptures. Furthermore, as evidence that the New Testament writers and Jesus had great respect for the Old Testament, they make many references to principles expounded in the older Scriptures. We will explore some of these references. Moreover, in the chapters on prophecy and types, we have also seen examples of consistency. Prophecies about Jesus Christ and other prophecies in the Old Testament were fulfilled in the New Testament, and Old Testament types foreshadowed Jesus Christ in the New Testament. To demonstrate these principles, I will address a number of areas of consistency such as New Testament references to Old Testament verses, the Law in the New Testament, the concept that all have sinned, the Trinity in the Old

Testament, and also very important, God's grace in the Old Testament. As with prophecy and typology, references are "salted and peppered" throughout the Bible.

NEW TESTAMENT REFERENCES
TO OLD TESTAMENT VERSES

According to Elwell and Comfort, "There are over 400 passages of the Old Testament that are explicitly cited in the New Testament."[1] Elwell and Comfort further state, "There are well over 1,000 places where there is an allusion to an Old Testament text, event, or person."[2] The New Testament writers were often referring to the *Scriptures* or *Scripture* to give credence to their explanations that Jesus was the Messiah foretold in the Old Testament. I found fifty-two verses in which the New Testament writers employed one of these terms. At the time of their writings, there was no New Testament as yet, and the Old Testament was known to all as the *Scriptures*. I found nine references by Jesus to the Scriptures. For example Luke 24:27 states, "And beginning with Moses and all the Prophets, he explained to them what was said in all the Scriptures concerning himself." I also found 153 verses referring to the Old Testament terms *Prophet* or *Prophets*.

I have selected a small representative number of verses where the New Testament writers refer to an Old Testament event. In Genesis 4, we read of the first murder in the Bible, that of Cain murdering his brother Abel. In 1 John 3:12, the author states, "Do not be like Cain, who belonged to the evil one and murdered his brother." Genesis 12 tells the story of God calling Abraham (then known as Abram) to leave his home and go to another land. God promises him that God will bless him and make a great nation from his offspring. The author of Hebrews refers to this event as follows: "By faith Abraham, when called to go to a place he would later receive as his inheritance, obeyed and went, even though he did not know where he was going" (Hebrews 11:8). The apostle Paul also referred to this occurrence in Galations 3:8, and the apostle Luke covers the same situation in Acts 3:24–26.

Many of us have heard the story of "Jonah and the whale." Actually, the Bible does not refer to a whale, but rather a large fish. As unlikely as it

---

1. Walter A. Elwell and Philip W. Comfort, *Tyndale Bible Dictionary,* Wheaton, IL: Tyndale House Publishers, 195.

2. Ibid., 196.

may seem that a large fish could swallow a man, could not the creator of the universe provide such a fish if he chose? The reason for this astounding event is because God called Jonah to go to Ninevah, the capital city of Assyria, to preach to the sinful Assyrians. This was so repulsive to Jonah that he rebelled and tried to escape to Spain. When a violent storm threatened to sink the ship, Jonah actually convinced the sailors to throw him overboard, because he knew that God had brought on the storm because of him. At first reluctant, the sailors complied and the fish did the rest. In the book of Matthew, it is actually Jesus' words that refer to Jonah: "He answered, 'A wicked and adulterous generation asks for a miraculous sign! But none will be given it except the sign of the prophet Jonah. For as Jonah was three days and three nights in the belly of a huge fish, so the Son of Man will be three days and three nights in the heart of the earth'" (Matthew 12:39–40).

Another famous story is the fall of Jericho, immortalized by the song, "Joshua fit the battle of Jericho, and the walls came tumblin' down." The Old Testament story is told in Joshua chapter six. Hebrews 11:30, in a passage about the faith of the Israelites, makes reference to this event: "By faith the walls of Jericho fell, after the people had marched around them for seven days."

THE LAW IN THE NEW TESTAMENT

Because of God's grace in the New Testament through Jesus Christ, there is a common misconception that the Law is negated in the New Testament. We shall see that the Law is still intact, but through Jesus' sacrifice, there is forgiveness available for our transgressions against the Law. I have selected a few of the many New Testament verses showing that the Law is still in effect.

Jesus said in Matthew 5:17–18, "Do not think that I have come to abolish the Law or the Prophets; I have not come to abolish them. I tell you the truth, until heaven and earth disappear, not the smallest letter, not the least stroke of a pen, will by any means disappear from the Law until everything is accomplished." In fact Jesus clarified the fundamental basis of the Law when he was confronted by a Pharisee who was testing him. The man asked Jesus which is the greatest commandment in the Law. Jesus surprised him by not selecting one of the ten commandments. Rather, he said to the man, "'Love the Lord your God with all your heart and with all your soul and with all your mind.' This is the first and greatest commandment. And the second is like it: 'Love your neighbor as yourself.' All the Law and the Prophets hang on these two commandments" (Matthew 22:37–40). The idea is that if we truly love God and mankind, our actions will fulfill the Law.

I counted 109 verses in the New Testament in which the apostle Paul expounded on the Law. In one example, Paul stated, "Do we, then, nullify the Law by this faith? Not at all! Rather, we uphold the Law" (Romans 3:31). Here again we have consistency between the testaments. The Law is not made obsolete in the New Testament. It is fulfilled and clarified by Jesus, Paul, and the other apostolic authors of New Testament books.

ALL HAVE SINNED

The concept of grace in the New Testament frequently involves expressions of mankind's sinfulness, with grace available for forgiveness. Paul states in Romans 3:23 a phrase often expressed in treatises on Christianity. It simply says, "For all have sinned and fall short of the glory of God . . ." But is this merely a New Testament concept? No, there are numerous Old Testament verses that are in agreement. I have again selected just a few to demonstrate the point.

Proverbs 20:9 rhetorically queries, "Who can say, 'I have kept my heart pure; I am clean and without sin'"? Then in Ecclesiastes 7:20, we read, "There is not a righteous man on earth who does what is right and never sins." There also are numerous examples in the Psalms. Psalm 14:3 tells us, "All have turned aside, they have together become corrupt; there is no one who does good, not even one." We also see in the Psalm 143:2, "Do not bring your servant into judgment, for no one living is righteous before you." Again we see consistency between Old and New Testament principles.

THE TRINITY IN THE OLD TESTAMENT

By the Trinity we mean the three personal aspects of the one true God. This is a very difficult concept for us earthly beings to assimilate. The term Trinity is not mentioned in the Bible, but it is clear from exploring all the Scriptures that God has three aspects: Father, Son, and Holy Spirit. It is also clear that the Father is expressed throughout the Bible, so I will not discuss his presence in both Testaments—it is not a controversial proposition. But how about the presence of Jesus and the Holy Spirit in the Old Testament? Jesus in the New Testament is also not a problem. He appears throughout. The New Testament is all about him. Let's see what the Scriptures tell us about the Trinity.

The first idea that there is a plural aspect to God comes up very early in the book of Genesis. After God created many creatures, he turned to the thought of creating mankind. In Genesis 1:26, he says, "Let *us* make man in *our* image, in *our* likeness . . . " (emphasis added). Note the use of plural nouns, *us* and *our* by God. From this reference, we cannot conclude that there is a trinity, only a plurality. We must explore further.

Can we find Jesus in the Old Testament? Well, we will not find him by name, but there are numerous references throughout the Old Testament to the Messiah, by various names and designations. In chapter three on prophecy, we saw that the fifty-third chapter of Isaiah had many details that only could pertain to Jesus Christ. Isaiah 9 also has a very interesting prophecy showing that a *Son* is equated to *Mighty God* and *Everlasting Father*. Here is a clear picture of the aspects of God. Verses 6–7 read:

For to us a child is born, to us a Son ers. And he will be called Wonderful Counselor, *Mighty God* (emphasis added), Everlasting Father, Prince of Peace.

> Of the increase of his government and peace there will be no end.
> He will reign on David's throne and over his kingdom, establishing
> and upholding it with justice and righteousness from that time on
> and forever. The zeal of the Lord Almighty will accomplish this.

Some very important factors emerge from these verses. As stated above, the Son is equated to Mighty God and Everlasting Father. We see that he will reign on David's throne . . . *forever*. No other descendant of David qualifies for an eternal throne. This is a future kingdom, and only Jesus fits all the requirements. When the angel comes to Mary to tell her she will give birth to Jesus, he says. "He will be great and will be called the Son of the Most High. The Lord God will give him the throne of his father David, and he will reign over the house of Jacob *forever*; his *kingdom will never end*" (emphasis added) (Luke 1:32–33). Additional verses in Isaiah refer to the Messiah being a descendant of Jesse, David's father, along with other prophecies about the Messiah (Isaiah 11:1–5). Moreover, we have in Isaiah 7:14 the famous passage predicting the virgin birth of the Messiah.

The Psalms also record many references to the Messiah. One important reference is contained in Psalm 110:1. This Psalm is one of many written by David, a prolific composer. Psalm 110 is a prophecy about the eventual kingdom of the Messiah, and verse one says, "The Lord says to my Lord: 'Sit at my right hand until I make your enemies a footstool for your feet.'" Jesus challenges the Pharisees in Matthew 22:41–46 as to what this verse meant. The Pharisees admit that the Christ or Messiah is the son of David. Jesus points out in the Psalm David refers to his Lord, ergo his son, at the right hand of God. The Pharisees are speechless, as Jesus is commonly called, Son of David. (Note the term, *son of*, was commonly used for any descendant of an individual, not only that person's immediate child. Jesus lived generations after David.) This passage is also present in Mark and Luke. Peter also expounds on this verse in Acts 2:34–36, explaining that "God has made this Jesus, whom you crucified, both Lord and Christ."

In the passage discussed above, in Isaiah 9, the term Wonderful Counselor refers to the Holy Spirit. In John 14:26, Jesus states "But the Counselor, the Holy Spirit, whom the Father will send in my name, will teach you all things and will remind you of everything I have said to you." So, the Isaiah 9 passage refers to all three persons of the Trinity. I counted 177 verses in the Old Testament that refer to the Spirit of God, or Holy Spirit. I will cite just a few examples. Nehemiah 9:20 states, "You gave your good Spirit to instruct them," and in verse 30, we find, "For many years you were patient with them. By your Spirit you admonished them through your prophets." After his adultery with Bathsheba, David makes a petition to God in Psalm 51:11, "Do not cast me from your presence or take your Holy Spirit from me."

GOD'S GRACE IN THE OLD TESTAMENT

Webster's Dictionary describes grace as being "unmerited divine assistance given man for his regeneration or sanctification."[3] More simply, grace has also been defined as "unmerited favor." Does God provide grace in the Old Testament? Many have thought that the Bible expounds two distinctly different tenets: obedience to the Law in the Old Testament and salvation by grace in the New Testament. To a degree the two major divi-

---

3. *Webster's Seventh New Collegiate Dictionary.* Springfield, MA: G. & C. Merriam Co., 1972, 362.

sions of the Bible have such emphases. However, if the Bible is totally inspired by God, would we not expect his grace to also be revealed in the Old Testament? Similarly, Jesus and the New Testament writers make it clear that the Law has not become obsolete. I give a number of examples of God's grace in the Old Testament. The nation of Israel and a number of important Old Testament personages, such as Nehemiah, David, and Daniel implore God to grant his grace; and he does.

Because of evil in Israel in the Old Testament, God could have permanently rejected his chosen people. His pain at their disrespecting him and pursuing other gods is evident over and over and over again in the Old Testament scriptures. As one reads the historical Old Testament books, it is clear the chosen people often turn their backs on their God. One has only to read the books of the prophets to hear the anguish in the words of the Lord as he expresses the hurts he has experienced. However, his message to them continuously throughout the Old Testament is to repent and there will be blessings. Continuing to reject him and committing evil will have negative consequences. God's love and patience are incredible. No matter what evil his people committed, he is quick to forgive if they repent and return to him. Observe his words in Malachi 3:7, "Ever since the time of your forefathers you have turned away from my decrees and have not kept them. Return to me, and I will return to you, 'says the Lord Almighty." Very similar words appear in Zechariah 1:3.

It is also appropriate at this point to emphasize that I am not singling out Israel as a culprit nation. We see from all history, and especially in the New Testament that all persons sin and disappoint our Creator. We shall see in chapter seven on the basics how God provided a way for sinners to become acceptable to God.

A very repetitive cycle in the Old Testament consists of the following steps:

1. Israel enjoys blessings from God.

2. After a period of time, Israel lapses into sinful behavior such as following the sinful practices of the neighboring nations, worshipping idols, sacrificing their firstborn children, etc.

3. God withdraws blessings and allows Israel to be conquered by enemy nations.

4. Israel repents and cries out to God to help them.

5. God forgives them, provides a conquering hero to rescue them, and then restores blessings.

6. The cycle repeats itself.

Let's look at an example in the book of Judges:

> The Israelites did evil in the eyes of the Lord; they forgot the Lord their God and served the Baals and the Asherahs. (Author's note: These were gods worshipped by neighboring peoples.) The anger of the Lord burned against Israel so that he sold them into the hands of Cushan-Rishathaim king of Aram Naharaim, to whom the Israelites were subject for eight years. But when they cried out to the Lord, he raised up for them a deliverer, Othniel son of Kenaz, Caleb's younger brother, who saved them (Judges 3:7–9).

This cycle was repeated many times in the book of Judges. But did God's grace ever wear out? No. Throughout the Old Testament, we see God beseeching his people to repentance by means of the prophets. When they turned back from their sins, he forgave them and restored blessings.

One of the Lord's favorite persons was David. The Messiah, Jesus Christ, was to come from David's lineage. God referred to David as a man after his own heart. Was that because David was sinless? No, David was a sinner who committed terrible transgressions. He coveted Bathsheba, a married woman, and committed adultery with her. When it was learned she was pregnant, and the father could not be her husband Uriah, who was away at war, David conspired to bring Uriah home to sleep with his wife. The honorable Uriah refused to do so while his compatriots were away in battle. He went back to the front lines, not knowing David had ordered that he be assigned to a position where he would be killed. When the prophet Nathan confronted David, he repented in great sorrow for what he had done, and God forgave him. Psalm 51 is a lengthy confession of his sins and his pleas to God for forgiveness, However, although he was forgiven, there were consequences to his sins—for example, the baby died. Psalm 32 is another Psalm by David expressing the concept of grace in the Old Testament. Here are the opening verses of this Psalm: "Blessed is he whose transgressions are forgiven, whose sins are covered. Blessed is the man whose sin the Lord does not count against him and in whose spirit is no deceit" (Psalm 32:1–2); and again in verse 5: "Then I acknowledged my sin to you and did not cover up my iniquity. I said, 'I will confess my transgressions to the Lord'—and you forgave the guilt of my sin." I can cite many other verses that show God's grace in the Old Testament—many other instances to show that grace is present equally in both testaments.

This chapter on consistency in the two Testaments is vital evidence. It could be so easy to have conflicting principles throughout the 66 books of the Bible. Rather, there is remarkable agreement, as we have seen by the words of Jesus citing Old Testament principles and fulfillment of prophecy. Furthermore, the New Testament authors, show over and over again that their writings substantiate what was known at the time as "The Scriptures," or Old Testament. God's inspiration infused all of the writers throughout the Bible. What other religious document can hold up to the Bible? What other religious document has so many authors who substantiate each other?

Part Three
The Bible's Plan for Eternal Life

7

The Basics

For God so loved the world, that he gave his one and only Son, that whoever believes in him shall not perish, but have eternal life.

John 3:16

IN PREVIOUS CHAPTERS OF this book, elements of the basics of the Gospel have been discussed. In this chapter, I will tie it all together systematically. The goal of this chapter is to present briefly some important concepts, especially for those who have not had extensive exposure to these topics. First, I explain what the most important topic that any of us can consider, the Gospel, is all about. Then I talk about variations in the belief systems of those who call themselves Christians, followed by a short section on works.

THE GOSPEL

Definition

After having considered the existence of a Creator, how he chooses to communicate with mankind, and the manual that he left us, *The Bible*, it is important to deal with the concept of how we can be made acceptable before God. Do we earn acceptance through doing good deeds? Or is there another way? Therefore, at this point it is appropriate to discuss the Gospel of Christ, because it is the way *The Bible* clearly states is the way to eternal life with God. For persons who are Christians and are reading this work to strengthen their faith, this section is already well understood by them. However, for other readers who may not be believers, my aim is to provide logical information upon which they can base their decision.

The word *Gospel* is derived from the Anglo-Saxon *godspell* meaning glad tidings or good news.[1] The latter term is most often used to define "Gospel." The apostle Paul even refers to the Gospel pertaining to Abraham in the Old Testament (Galatians 3:8). Gospel is a term sprinkled throughout the New Testament, the noun appearing 54 times.[2] But what is the good news? The good news is that God has provided salvation, or eternal life, through the incarnation, life, death, and resurrection of his Son, Jesus Christ.[3] The good news is that Jesus has come and salvation is at hand. Our responsibility is to accept the gift and live a life of repentance.

Salvation is a Gift, not Earned

John the Baptist was the forerunner of Jesus Christ. In Mark 1:4, John comes baptizing in the desert "and preaching a baptism of repentance for the forgiveness of sins." Note that he is not preaching that one should decrease bad works and increase good works so the good will outweigh the bad. The latter is the basis of many other religions, but it is not God's way. The key words in the passage are *repentance*—literally, a change of one's attitude toward God—and *forgiveness of sins*. In Ephesians 2:8–10, the apostle Paul tells us, "For it is by grace you have been saved, through faith—and this not from yourselves, it is the gift of God—not by works, so that no one can boast." Again, it is not outweighing sins with good works, but rather, wiping the slate clean. Salvation is not a reward for human effort, but a gift from God, or *God's grace*.

Character of God

Why are repentance and forgiveness necessary? To answer this question, we need to understand something of the character of God. In Exodus 15:11, it states, "Who among the gods is like you, O Lord? Who is like you—majestic in holiness, awesome in glory, working wonders?" The prophet Habakkuk says of God: "Your eyes are too pure to look on evil;

1. Walter A. Elwell, Ph.D. and Philip W. Comfort, Ph.D., Editors, *Tyndale Bible Dictionary*, Wheaton, IL: Tyndale House Publishers, 2001, 546.

2. Ibid., 547.

3. Kenneth Barker, Editor, *The NIV Bible*, Grand Rapids: Zondervan Publishing House, 1985, 1493, footnote on Mark 1:1.

you cannot tolerate wrong" (Habakkuk 1:13). Moreover, 1 Peter 1:15–16 proclaims, "But just as he who called you is holy, so be holy in all you do; for it is written: 'Be holy, because I am holy.'" Peter is quoting God's statements in the Old Testament (Leviticus 11:44–45, 19:2). Finally, Hebrews 12:14 states, "Without holiness no one will see the Lord." What does it mean to be holy? The word literally means to be *set apart*. It eventually came to mean "spiritually pure, sacred, untainted by evil, sinless."[4] Because of God's holiness, or purity, he cannot coexist with sin. But the Bible also states in Romans 3:23, "All have sinned and fall short of the glory of God." How then can one who carries the burden of his/her sin be acceptable to the God who is holy? No amount of good works can offset the stain of the sin each of us has committed. That is where the sacrifice of Jesus on the cross comes in. He took our sin upon himself to present us acceptable to the holy God. As Ingram states, "God will not compromise his holiness, but through Christ, he satisfied it."[5] All we need to do is accept his gift.

A Sign from God

When Jesus died, God gave all of humanity a significant sign. In Exodus 26:31–33, we read the description of a curtain in the temple that separated the Holy Place from the Most Holy Place. Once a year, on the Day of Atonement, the high priest went into the Most Holy Place to perform the sacrifice for the sin of the people, so they would be forgiven. At the moment of Jesus' death, we read in Matthew 27:51, Mark 15:38, and Luke 23:45 that the curtain was torn from top to bottom. Jesus' sacrifice supplanted that of the high priest. No longer was the believer separated from God's presence by sin. The believer could now directly approach God in prayer.

Scriptural Evidence

The concept of God's grace is not merely contained in a verse or two in the Bible. It is pervasive. As we have seen in Chapter Six, the concept of God's grace begins in the Old Testament. In the sections to follow, I include many verses indicating the principle of salvation through the forgiveness of sins. I present these verses to demonstrate that salvation permeates all of the New Testament, and is critical to acceptance by God for eternal

4. Chip Ingram, *God as He Longs for You to See Him*, Grand Rapids: Baker Books, 2004. 105.

5. Ibid., 116,

life with him. Verses are from the books written by Matthew, Mark, Luke, John, Paul, and Peter. A number of the verses are quotations of Jesus' own words. I urge every reader to carefully peruse these verses. Look them up in your Bible. Check out the context of the statements. Nothing can be more important than understanding what these verses mean and making an appropriate decision about them. Because there are so many verses on this subject, I have selected a few to include in this section to illustrate the message of the Gospel. I have limited the selection so there would not be a long progression of verses. I have placed the references to many additional verses in Appendix A, *What Did Jesus Say?* and Appendix B, *What Did the Apostles and Others Say?* for those who want to dig deeper. The verses in the appendices are just as important as the ones that appear in this chapter. I encourage all readers to carefully consider the passages in the appendices.

What Did Jesus Say?

On His Deity

John 8:58–59: "'I tell you the truth,' Jesus answered, 'before Abraham was born, I am!' At this, they picked up stones to stone him, but Jesus hid himself, slipping away from the temple grounds." (Author's note: This statement was considered blasphemy, because "I Am" is one of the titles of God. That is why they wanted to stone him. They knew that he was claiming to be one with God.)

John 10:30–33: "'I and the Father are one.' Again the Jews picked up stones to stone him, but Jesus said to them, 'I have shown you many great miracles from the Father. For which of these do you stone me?' 'We are not stoning you for any of these,' replied the Jews, 'but for blasphemy, because you a mere man, claim to be God.'"

John 14:6: "Jesus answered, 'I am the way and the truth and the life. No one comes to the Father except through me.'"

Author's note: There is no question that Jesus was declaring his deity. He was equating himself with the Father. The people understood that clearly. Otherwise, why would they attempt to stone him? They considered what he said to be blasphemy, an offense punishable by stoning. Moreover, his words contradict the popular notion that all religions lead to God. Some may feel that this statement is narrow-minded. But once again, it was Jesus who said it, so it would be foolhardy to ignore it. Many say that Jesus was a great teacher, but not divine. They selectively choose from his teachings; for example, the Beatitudes, to live by. However, they neglect some of his most important teachings about his deity and his role as Savior. If he were a great teacher, we cannot select some teachings and reject others. We must accept all of his teachings as great.

His Role as Savior

Matthew 20:28: "Just as the Son of Man did not come to be served, but to serve, and to give his life as a ransom for many."

Mark 16:15–16: "Go into all the world and preach the good news to all creation. Whoever believes and is baptized will be saved, but whoever does not believe will be condemned."

Luke 15:10: "In the same way, I tell you, there is rejoicing in the presence of the angels of God over one sinner who repents."

Luke 24:46–47: "This is what is written: the Christ will suffer and rise from the dead on the third day, and repentance and forgiveness of sins will be preached in his name to all nations, beginning at Jerusalem."

John 3:3: "Jesus answered and said to him; 'Truly, truly, I say to you, unless one is born again, he cannot see the kingdom of God.'"

John 3:7: "You should not be surprised at my saying, 'You must be born again.'" (Author's Note: We often hear the term *born again Christian* used in the media and other sources. *Born again* has even made it into secular use to indicate someone who has improved his or her situation, such as a born again politician, author, athlete, etc. The term born again Christian is often used as a pejorative, because many people do not understand its origin or its meaning. As we see in the previous two verses, it was Jesus himself who originated the term. If Jesus said it, should we not take it seriously?)

John 3:14–15: "Just as Moses lifted up the snake in the desert, so the Son of Man must be lifted up, that everyone who believes in him may have eternal life."

John 3:16: "For God so loved the world that he gave his one and only Son, that whoever believes in him shall not perish but have eternal life." (Author's Note: This verse is often referred to as "the Gospel in a nutshell.")

John 3:17–18: "For God did not send his son into the world to condemn the world, but to save the world through him. Whoever believes in him is not condemned, but whoever does not believe stands condemned already because he has not believed in the name of God's one and only Son."

John 6:40: "For this is the will of my Father, that every one who beholds the Son and believes in him, may have eternal life, and I myself will raise him up on the last day."

John 10:27–28: "My sheep listen to my voice; I know them, and they follow me. I give them eternal life, and they shall never perish; no one can snatch them out of my hand."

What Did the Apostle Paul Say?

I include many verses by the apostle Paul, because he wrote a large number of New Testament books and was one of the best expositors of the Gospel. It would be of great value to the reader to read the first 10 chapters of the book of Romans. Another important selection, too lengthy to include in this section, is from Colossians 1:13–23, stated in its entirety in Appendix B.

Acts 13:38–39: "Therefore, my brothers, I want you to know that through Jesus the forgiveness of sins is proclaimed to you. Through him everyone who believes is justified from everything you could not be justified from by the Law of Moses."

Acts 16:31: "Believe in the Lord Jesus, and you will be saved—you and your household."

Romans 1:16: "For I am not ashamed of the gospel, for it is the power of God for salvation to everyone who believes, to the Jew first and also to the Greek."

Romans 3:23–24: "For all have sinned and fall short of the glory of God, and are justified freely by his grace through the redemption that came by Christ Jesus."

Romans 5:8: "But God demonstrates his own love for us in this: While we were still sinners, Christ died for us."

Romans 6:23: "For the wages of sin is death; but the gift of God is eternal life through Jesus Christ our Lord."

Romans 8:1: "Therefore, there is now no condemnation for those who are in Christ Jesus."

Romans 10:9–10: "That if you confess with your mouth, 'Jesus is Lord,' and believe in your heart that God raised him from the dead, you will be saved. For it is with your heart that you believe and are justified, and it is with your mouth that you confess and are saved."

Ephesians 2:8–9: "For it is by grace you are saved, through faith—and this not from yourselves, it is the gift of God—not by works, so that no one can boast."

1 Thessalonians 5:9–10: "For God did not appoint us to suffer wrath but to receive salvation through our Lord Jesus Christ. He died for us so that, whether we are awake or asleep, we may live together with him."

What Did the Apostle Peter Say?

Another important section relating to Jesus' role is cited in three of the gospels, Matthew 16:13–19; Mark 8:27–29; and Luke 9:18–20. Jesus asks his disciples, "Who do people say that the Son of Man is?" "Son of Man" is one of Jesus' titles, one that he particularly liked. A few of the disciples mentioned a number of opinions that people had given. Jesus asks the disciples who they (the disciples) say that he is. Peter answered, "You are the Christ, the Son of the Living God." Jesus praises him, because it had been revealed to Peter by the Father in heaven.

Acts 2:38: "Repent and be baptized, every one of you, in the name of Jesus Christ for the forgiveness of your sins."

Acts 4:12: (Author's note—Peter is referring to Jesus here): "Salvation is found in no one else, for there is no other name under heaven given to men by which we must be saved."

Acts 10:43: "All the prophets testify about him that everyone who believes in him receives forgiveness of sins through his name."

Acts 15:11: "We believe it is through the grace of our Lord Jesus that we are saved,"

1 Peter 2:24–25: "He himself bore our sins in his body on the tree, so that we might die to sins and live for righteousness; by his wounds you have been healed. For you were like sheep going astray, but now you have returned to the Shepherd and Overseer of your souls."

What Did the Apostle John Say?

John 1:12: "But as many as received him, to them he gave power to become sons of God, even to them that believe on his name."

John 20:31: "But these are written that you may believe that Jesus is the Christ, the Son of God, and that by believing you may have life in his name.

1 John 1:7–10: "But if we walk in the light, as he is in the light, we have fellowship with one another, and the blood of Jesus his Son, purifies us from all sin. If we claim to be without sin, we deceive ourselves and the truth is not in us. If we confess our sins, he is faithful and just and will forgive us our sins and purify us from all unrighteousness."

1 John 2:2: "He is the atoning sacrifice for our sins, and not only for ours but also for the sins of the whole world."

1 John 3:16: "This is how we know what love is: Jesus Christ laid down his life for us."

1 John 3:23: "And this is his command: to believe in the name of his Son, Jesus Christ, and to love one another as he commanded us."

1 John 4:9–10: "This is how God showed his love among us: he sent his one and only Son into the world that we might live through him. This is love: not that we love God, but that he loved us and sent his Son as an atoning sacrifice for our sins."

1 John 5:11–13: "And this is the testimony: God has given us eternal life, and this life is in his Son. He who has the Son has life; he who does not have the Son of God does not have life. I write these things to you who believe in the name of the Son of God so that you may know that you have eternal life."

What Did Others Say?

John the Baptist

John 1:29: "The next day John saw Jesus coming toward him and said, 'Look, the Lamb of God, who takes away the sin of the world!'"

John 3:36: "He who believes in the Son has eternal life; but he who does not obey the Son shall not see life, but the wrath of God abides on him."

Angel of the Lord to Joseph

Matthew 1:21: "She will give birth to a son, and you are to give him the name Jesus, because he will save his people from their sins."

Angel of the Lord to the Shepherds

Luke 2:10–11: "But the angel said to them, 'Do not be afraid. I bring you good news of great joy that will be for all the people. Today in the town of David a Savior has been born to you; he is Christ the Lord.'"

CHRISTIANS

Definition

Next, we will address the subject of *Christians*. Who are "Christians? On the surface, this question sounds simplistic. Many persons call themselves Christians. Do not all persons who call themselves Christians have a right to that title? Although it sounds simplistic, you probably have heard the old expression, "If it walks like a duck, and it quacks like a duck, it most likely is a duck." So how do we define a Christian? Well, if one talks the talk and walks the walk, that is a step in the right direction, but is it sufficient?

Talking the Talk

By talking the talk, we mean that one must be a believer in Jesus Christ, and accept his teachings—not many of his teachings, but all of them. Many persons accept some of Jesus' teachings. They say he was a great teacher, but they fall short of accepting him as the Christ (or Messiah), the sacrifice for our sins. Belief in the Jesus as Savior as contained in God's word, the Bible, should be the identifying mark of people who call themselves Christians.

Unfortunately, many persons who identify themselves as Christians do so for reasons other than belief in the Gospel or the Bible. Some persons identify themselves as Christians because they are not Jews, Muslims, Buddhists, etc. They may have no strong religious beliefs at all or affiliation with any church. Others may go to churches where the Gospel is not presented and is not part of the life of the attendees of the church. Such churches often stress moral living, certainly worthwhile teachings, but not the truths of the Gospel. In my early years, I attended such a church, which was a member of a mainline Protestant denomination. In that church, many Biblical stories were taught in Sunday school. Jesus was presented as a great teacher of morality, but not the Savior for the forgiveness of sins. It is important to understand these distinctions, because many sins have been committed in the name of Christianity, and would certainly have been denounced by Jesus.

Walking the Walk

Secondly, if one observes so-called "Christian behavior," it is important that the person be a true believer in the gospel of Christ, often termed an "evangelical Christian."

It is not a logical process to observe the behavior of what might be termed a "nominal Christian" (a description that is sometimes used to distinguish one from an evangelical Christian), and attribute the behavior as typically Christian. Such observations have often turned people who are unaware of this distinction from accepting the Gospel. I have had conversations with unbelievers who experienced a nominal Christian's behavior, and concluded that the behavior was "un-Christian."

Unfortunately, there is another inhibiting factor that can be ascribed to some evangelical Christians causing others to reject the Gospel. It must be pointed out that evangelical Christians are not perfect, but are forgiven. One's acceptance of Christ as Savior is the beginning of a long process of spiritual growth, termed *sanctification*. In the cases of many Christians, the point where they accept Christ is a great turning point, the point of *justification*. Friends notice a significant change in the person's life. Even such persons, whose lives turn around in amazing ways, are not perfect, but are on the path of sanctification. We must also recognize that in a number of cases, there is not an immediate great turn-around, but a more gradual process takes place as the Holy Spirit works in the new Christian's life.

I am reminded of a concert I attended many years ago, when one of my daughters played in the Junior High School orchestra. While I was very proud of the enthusiasm and commitment she and her fellow students displayed, let's face it; they were not the San Francisco Symphony. In fact, one might conclude Beethoven was a terrible composer! However, we know that when the notes are played properly, we appreciate Beethoven as a great composer. In fact, as these same students continue to learn and practice, they may aspire to be in a top symphony orchestra and play great music. It is like that with the Christian life. Often, as new Christians, we may not lead perfect lives, and observers may think God is not a great composer. However, as we continue our sanctification process through prayer, reading God's word, and serving our fellow man, we develop into better Christians, and persons who may be a very positive witness to God's grace. I state these factors so that seekers will be tolerant of the imperfections they may see in the lives of evangelical Christians hoping the seeker will give consideration to the Gospel message. The message may even be conveyed by a friend who is not perfect, but is truly concerned for the eternal welfare of his or her friend.

Note that being an evangelical Christian has nothing to do with denominations, Protestantism, Roman Catholicism, etc. It applies to all who have accepted Jesus Christ as Savior, independent of the labels we have chosen for our spiritual associates. As will be seen in the two chapters on "Transformed Lives," this way is open to persons of all backgrounds. In Galatians 3:26–29 it says, "You are all sons of God through faith in Christ Jesus, for all of you who were baptized into Christ have clothed yourselves with Christ. There is *neither Jew nor Greek, slave nor free, male nor female, for you are all one in Christ Jesus* (emphasis added). If you belong to Christ, then you are Abraham's seed, and heirs according to the promise."

Christ or Messiah?

Another important point is that Christians were not always called Christians! The name was given to the believers in Antioch of Syria; long after Jesus was crucified, resurrected, and ascended into Heaven. Christ is the Greek term for the Hebrew word, Mashiach (or Messiah). The term Christ has become dominant, because the New Testament was written primarily in Greek. Some may think that Christ is Jesus' last name. It is not. It is his title. Christ (Greek) or Meshiach (Hebrew) means *anointed*.[6]

Sometimes I consider it unfortunate that we use the Greek version of Messiah (the anglicized term), because an important fact is sometimes lost. The Christian church was not started as a Gentile reaction to Judaism. It was started by Jews. Jesus was a Jew. His apostles were Jews. Christianity is really the natural extension of Judaism, as prophesied extensively in the Old Testament. Moreover, the apostle Paul in Romans 11:17–24 is teaching Gentiles that they are like wild olive branches grafted on to the main

6. Moishe Rosen, *Y'shua*, Chicago: Moody Press, 1982, 1.

olive tree root. In the Bible, the olive tree is often utilized as a symbol of Israel. In other words, Gentile Christians have been grafted on to the main line of Judaism. In Romans 1:16, Paul tells us, "I am not ashamed of the Gospel, because it is the power of God for the salvation of everyone who believes: *first for the Jew* (emphasis added), then for the Gentile. And yet, the names Christian and Christianity can be obstacles to dialog between Christians and Jews because of some the unfortunate history ascribed to the term Christianity.

My heart goes out to the Jews of today, especially the orthodox Jews who await their Messiah. How would he be different from Jesus Christ? How would he fulfill the many prophecies that Jesus did? How would they know that he is from the lineage of David? The list goes on and on. One stumbling block in the way of accepting Jesus as Messiah is that historically Jews expected one who would become a righteous ruler, overthrowing Roman rule, and restoring the kingdom of Israel. However, what has been ignored by those who do not accept Jesus is that the prophets wrote that he would come first as "the suffering servant," as seen in Isaiah 53, who would be crucified for the sins of mankind. Jesus will return to establish his kingdom on earth. The chapter on prophecy also touched on this subject.

Works

If we did not consider the role of works or good deeds, a distorted view of Christianity might be the result. Works do not justify one with God. Works do not save one. Works do not provide eternal life. As discussed above, trust in Jesus as Savior provides one with eternal life or salvation. However, the Bible also provides direction to the believer about works. In the book of Ephesians, the apostle Paul teaches, "For we are God's workmanship, created in Christ Jesus to do good works, which God prepared in advance for us to do" (Ephesians 2:10). The apostle James queries, "What good is it, my brothers, if a man claims to have faith but has no deeds?" (James 2:14). He adds, "In the same way, faith by itself, if it is not accompanied by action, is dead" (James 2:17).

Jesus also taught about good works. He came to save mankind, but he still preached messages of love and service. One of His most famous parables dealt with works. In Luke 10:30–37, Jesus responds to a question with the parable of the "Good Samaritan:"

A man was going down from Jerusalem to Jericho, when he fell into the hands of robbers. They stripped him of His clothes, beat him and went away, leaving him half dead. A priest happened to be going down the same road, and when he saw the man, he passed by on the other side. So too, a Levite, when he came to the place and saw him, passed by on the other side. But a Samaritan, as he traveled, came where the man was; and when he saw him, he took pity on him. He went to him and bandaged his wounds, pouring on oil and wine. Then he put the man on his own donkey, took him to an inn and took care of him. The next day he took out two silver coins and gave them to the innkeeper. "Look after him," he said, "and when I return, I will reimburse you for any extra expense you may have." Which of these three do you think was a neighbor to the man who fell into the hands of robbers? The expert in the law replied, "The one who had mercy on him." Jesus told him, "Go and do likewise."

It is especially noteworthy that the self-righteous elite ones in the story, the priest and the Levite, did not help the victim. Jesus chose a Samaritan, hated by the Jews, as the hero of the story, again indicating his inclusiveness for all who are his. God has a plan for each life. The first step is to accept Jesus as Savior. God then brings about his purposes through the services performed by his people.

RECOMMENDED READING

John R.W. Stott, *Basic Christianity*, Grand Rapids: Eerdmans Publishing Co., 1958.

C. S. Lewis, *Mere Christianity*, New York: Macmillan Publishing Co., 1943.

Part Four
More Evidence

8

Transformed Lives—The Apostles

Do not conform any longer to the pattern of this world, but be transformed by the renewing of your mind. Then you will be able to test and approve what God's will is—his good, pleasing and perfect will.

Romans 12:2

ANOTHER IMPORTANT BODY OF evidence for the Gospel of Jesus Christ is the phenomenon of transformed lives. Adherents of other belief systems can tell of changed lives also. Usually they will relate how their belief system has brought them peace, a sense of well-being, or new friends. The difference in Christianity is an important one. In this case, the change does not come from human power or a change of human circumstance. Rather, as Jesus taught just before his crucifixion, the person is transformed by the power of the Holy Spirit that enters his or her life when they accept Jesus as their Savior. There is a major change in the direction of the person's life.

It has been estimated that there are 60 to 70 million evangelical Christians in the United States alone.[1] Every one of these individuals represents a transformed life, a story about a before and an after. Most can remember how their conversion came about, although decades may have passed since the event took place. It might have been a friend or coworker, relating how he or she came to be a Christian. Perhaps it was attending a church service or a Christian "crusade." Some have been enmeshed in such extremely dire straits, that they took to reading the Bible, and learned of their need for forgiveness and salvation. There are many

---

1. CBSNews.com, February 8, 2004; Isi Leibler, *Evangelical Christians, Our New Allies*, Jerusalem Post, August 15, 2003.

ways in which individuals hear about God's grace and desire to forgive them of their sins.

However they have come to the Lord, the changes are often immediately dramatic, because of the power of the Holy Spirit creating major changes in the person's life. Spouses, other family members, and friends are often astounded by the positive changes they witness in their friend or loved one. Some transformations are very exciting. Many have been rescued from drug abuse, alcoholism, or other addictions. Some have been involved in crime. However, others have had less dramatic conversions, simply recognizing the sin in their lives and their need for forgiveness. But in all cases, there is a recognizable change in direction, from one of self-interest to that of pleasing God.

ELEVEN NOT SO ORDINARY MEN

Selection & Characteristics

The title for this section is an enigma. The eleven men I am talking about are the original apostles, Judas Iscariot excluded. They started off ordinary, but became extraordinary. They were not highly educated men, nor of any elite class. Four of them were fishermen. One of them was a hated tax collector. Tax collectors were the "leeches" of Jewish society. They worked for the Roman government, and had defined amounts they were responsible to furnish to the government. However, many of them were corrupt and collected huge amounts, pocketing the overages. Why would Jesus select a tax collector? You will get the answer shortly.

The professions of the others remain unknown. Jesus even chose Judas Iscariot among the original twelve, probably because he knew Judas would betray him, triggering the progression to the cross and fulfilling prophecy. The apostles were not selected suddenly. Many had followed Jesus in the early days of his three-year ministry. Some of them had been disciples of John the Baptist, looking forward to the arrival of the Messiah. Jesus had prior interactions with some of them, and at the appropriate time, he assembled the twelve (Luke 6:13–16).

What in the world did Jesus see in them? Jesus could have chosen men with criteria we would consider far more suitable. There were the educated Pharisees, Sadducees, Teachers of the Law, Scribes, and numerous other leaders and elite persons. He could have selected merchants or other individuals with intelligence and business acumen. Ah, but fortunately, we were not the ones doing the choosing. As I described in detail in chapter five, God's ways are different than man's ways. We saw that God often chose persons who would be considered "weak vessels," doing mighty deeds through them for his purposes and his glory. I believe Jesus was able to look past the apostles' obvious shortcomings to what they would become after his ascension, and after they received the power of the Holy Spirit. He no doubt knew the potential of their character, their eventual leadership, and their commitment.

The selection of the apostles took place about halfway through Jesus' ministry. The training was intensive. They were together with Jesus constantly. They heard his sermons to the multitudes. They heard him preach in the synagogues. They witnessed many miracles. They heard his sophisticated replies to the Jewish leadership that were often trying to trap him. He explained the meaning of parables to them. And yet, early on, the apostles appeared simple, unable to grasp elementary principles. They often exasperated Jesus; often just not getting it. They squabbled among themselves, drawing rebukes from Jesus. At times they feared for their lives. In one case, they were with Jesus in a boat, crossing a lake. Jesus was asleep. A storm arose and threatened to capsize the boat. In dread, they awakened Jesus, who chastised them for their lack of faith.

Preparation

As they moved towards Jerusalem and Jesus' appointment with the cross, Jesus began to prepare the apostles for his death (Luke 17:22–25). As reported in the Gospels, Matthew, Mark, and Luke, Jesus is very specific in telling them that he will be betrayed to the chief priests and the teachers of the law. Speaking of himself, he says, "They will condemn him to death and will turn him over to the Gentiles to be mocked and flogged and crucified. On the third day he will be raised to life" (Matthew 20:18–19). In Luke 18:34, we learn that the disciples did not understand any of this, and they did not know what he was talking about. A short time later, he again alludes to his impending crucifixion (John 12:32–33). At this stage, it is apparent that Jesus has been very lucid about what is coming. We might have expected that the apostles would be prepared and ready for what was to follow. Unfortunately, that was not the case.

Fear and Confusion

One of the most significant events in the New Testament involves the man, Simon Peter, who is destined to become one of the most important leaders of the early church. Jesus had given him the name Peter, which means "rock," in anticipation of what Peter would become. However, at the time of Jesus' capture and trial, Peter was anything but a rock. During his final meal with the apostles, Jesus instituted the sacrament of Communion, and he was continuing to tell them what would come about. He predicted they all would fall away, as prophesied in the Old Testament by the prophet Zechariah (Zechariah 13:7). Peter, who was a blustery, volatile, outspoken man claimed that he would never fall away. Jesus then declared, before the rooster crowed, Peter would deny him three times. After Judas led the captors to Jesus, he was taken to meetings with the former high priest, then to the current high priest for inquisitions. In the courtyard, Peter was accused three times by bystanders of being an associate of Jesus. He denied vigorously each accusation. Just then the rooster crowed. The account in the Gospel of Luke says that Jesus looked straight at Peter. Matthew, Mark, and Luke all report that Peter wept bitterly.

The other disciples also fell away, as predicted by Jesus. One of the disciples "fled naked" (Mark 14:51). Mark is the only Gospel author who reports this incident, and most scholars believe this person is Mark himself. It is fascinating that he has the humility to write about his own failing. During the many years between the time of his flight and his writing of the gospel, Mark had become a great missionary.

During the crucifixion, only one disciple is recorded being there, and that is the apostle John. His presence is only recorded in his Gospel (John 19:25–27). Jesus looked down from the cross and told Mary that John was now her son. He then told John that Mary was now his mother. The Gospel records that John took Mary into his home. It is interesting that the Gospels record many of the women followers were at the crucifixion. Only John among the disciples is mentioned. After his death, Jesus was taken down from the cross and placed in a tomb.

Again, unlike typical expositions at the time of Christ, which rarely mentioned women, who were considered lowly, the Bible shows they were prominent in the resurrection story. Mary Magdalene arrived at dawn to an empty tomb and ran to tell Peter and John. Other women arrived, and an angel sent them to tell the disciples. Where were the men? John reports,

"On the evening of that first day of the week, when the disciples were together, with the doors locked for fear of the Jews" (John 20:19). Note that they were afraid for their lives. Eventually, Peter and John also ran to the tomb. As John reported in his Gospel, "They still did not understand from Scripture that Jesus had to rise from the dead" (John 30:9). Again, a Gospel author humbly reports his own shortcoming.

The Holy Spirit and Transformation

Up to now, the disciples and apostles have shown fear and confusion. As we will see, a great change comes over all of them. What was the cause or causes for such dramatic changes in these men? I believe the answer is there were at least two causes. Certainly, the appearances of Jesus after the resurrection, extensively reported in the Gospels, had an effect. The Gospels tell us that Jesus made appearances to many people, especially including the disciples and apostles, over a 40-day period. An excellent example of a transformation occurs in the apostle Thomas. During one of Jesus' meetings with the disciples, Thomas was not present. When he was told they had seen the Lord, he declared, "Unless I see the nail marks in his hands and put my finger where the nails were, and put my hand into his side, I will not believe it" (John 20:25). A week later, Jesus appears with Thomas present. He tells Thomas to "Put your finger here; see my hands. Reach out your hand and put it into my side. Stop doubting and believe." Thomas responds, " My Lord and my God!" (John 20:27–28).

Perhaps equally important was what took place at Pentecost. Pentecost was the time of the Festival of Weeks, celebrated 50 days after the Passover. Because of this festival, many believers were gathered in one place. The apostle Luke tells us in his New Testament book of Acts that just before Jesus ascended into heaven, he had told the apostles, in what is now termed the great commission: "But you will receive power when the Holy Spirit comes on you; and you will be my witnesses in Jerusalem, and in all Judea and Samaria, and to the ends of the earth" (Acts 1:8). As predicted by Jesus, the Holy Spirit descended upon the gathering at Pentecost. The Bible reports many miraculous activities occurring at the gathering, so there is some confusion among those present. Many had come from far off lands and did not know what was happening. Peter arose and addressed the crowd in a lengthy and detailed speech, and he explained how the prophet Joel in the Old Testament predicted the actions they were witnessing. This

uneducated man now had become an articulate speaker. He clearly had become the leader of the disciples, apostles, and the early church. And what of
"Doubting Thomas?" Tradition has it that he went east, where he founded
the first Christian church in Mesopotamia in 33 A.D., The Holy Apostolic
Catholic Assyrian Church of the East.[2] Other sources state he continued
eastward, conducting evangelism activity in India.

Now fearless and empowered, the apostles began carrying out the
great commission. We find Peter and John speaking to the public
about Jesus and his sacrifice for their sins. Great multitudes became believers. As a result, Peter and John were jailed by the priests, the temple
guards, and the Sanhedrin (the ruling body). These were the same culprits
responsible for the crucifixion. The apostles were jailed overnight and the
next day, the authorities questioned them. Peter courageously rebuked
them in a long dissertation. The rulers were amazed at the knowledge of
these uneducated men: "When they saw the courage of Peter and John
and realized they were unschooled, ordinary men, they were astonished
and they took note that these men had been with Jesus" (Acts 4:13). They
were commanded to stop all preaching. They refused. Arrested again,
an angel freed them. They continued preaching to the people and again
raised the ire of the Jewish leadership. They were seized and jailed again.
When an angel again freed them, they continued to preach.

The Sanhedrin wanted to put them to death. However, a reasonable
Pharisee, named Gamaliel, mentioned numerous other prior leaders who
faded away. He advised the rulers to ignore the apostles. "Therefore in
the present case I advise you: Leave these men alone! Let them go! For
if their purpose of activity is of human origin, it will fail. But if it is from
God, you will not be able to stop these men; you will only find yourselves
fighting against God" (Acts 5:38–39). The rulers had them flogged again
and freed them. Flogging was not to be taken lightly. It was an extremely
brutal torture!

In the interest of brevity, I will not go into more detail. To summarize
this section, we had eleven "ordinary men" who became extraordinary
men. These fearful men, who were in hiding before Pentecost, became
fearless. Along with other disciples, they courageously preached the
Gospel. Repeatedly forbidden to preach by the Sanhedrin, they defiantly
obeyed the mission given to them by the Lord. They were responsible for

2. Assyria Foundation Website, Assyrian Ancient History, www.assyriafoundation.org.

taking the Gospel throughout the mid-east. Matthew, the tax collector, and John wrote two of the Gospels. James and Peter wrote several New Testament epistles.

As indicated in the writings of early church scholars, all but the apostle John were martyred for their courage and faithfulness in preaching the gospel. John was exiled to the island of Patmos, where he wrote the book of Revelation. The words of Gamaliel above came true, although not in the manner he intended. Their mission was from God, and nothing the Jewish leadership could do was able to stop them. God blessed their faithfulness with dramatic growth of his church. They truly were great examples of lives transformed by God's Holy Spirit, and evidence of his power!

ONE EXTRAORDINARY MAN

The Antagonist

We first meet the apostle Paul, then called Saul, in the seventh chapter of the book of Acts. There was a large gathering of people who were enraged at one of the disciples named Stephen. He was very successful in presenting the Gospel and attracted the attention of the enemies of Jesus Christ. As with Jesus, these people had no legal grounds against Stephen, so they brought in false witnesses to make dishonest claims against him. Stephen gave a magnificent defense before the high priest and the Sanhedrin. He reviewed the history of the Jewish people, culminating in a stinging criticism of his oppressors. As a result, they dragged him out and stoned him to death. Acts 7:58 tells us, "Meanwhile, the witnesses laid their clothes at the feet of a young man named Saul" (later to be known as Paul). A few verses later, we read, "And Saul was there, giving approval to his death." We also learn that a great persecution broke out against the church at Jerusalem, and all but the apostles and disciples were scattered throughout Judea and Samaria. "But Saul began to destroy the church. Going from house to house, he dragged off men and women and put them in prison" (Acts 8:3).

Saul was not an ordinary man. He was a Jew of the tribe of Benjamin, one of the 12 tribes of Israel. However, he was not born in the confines of Israel. Rather, he was born in Tarsus, the capital city of the Roman province, Cilicia. Tarsus was an educational center with a full-fledged university and was known for the vocation of tent-making. After his conversion and during his later years of servanthood, this trade provided Paul with income as he ministered throughout the mid-east. His trade allowed him to be self-supporting wherever he traveled, and he did not draw resources from those he served. He was born a Roman citizen, which provided him with certain advantages at times when he was unfairly imprisoned or shackled.

He spoke Hebrew, Aramaic, and Greek. He was privileged to study under the Pharisee, Gamaliel, one of the most eminent teachers of the Hebrew Scriptures. According to Tyndale, "The learning of Gamaliel was so eminent and his influence so great that he is one of only seven Jewish scholars who have been honored by the title Rabban. He was called the 'Beauty of the Law.' The Talmud even says that 'since Rabban Gamaliel died, the glory of the Law has ceased.'"[3] This was the same Gamaliel who showed a measure of reason in the previous section.

Thus, Saul the Pharisee, the son of a Pharisee was schooled under a truly great educator. In his own words: "For you have heard of my previous way of life in Judaism, how intensely I persecuted the church of God and tried to destroy it. I was advancing in Judaism beyond many Jews of my own age and was extremely zealous for the traditions of my fathers" (Galations 1:13–14). He also said, "I persecuted the followers of this Way to their death, arresting both men and women and throwing them in prison" (Acts 22:4). Paul's persecution of the church was so pervasive that even after his conversion to Jesus Christ, Christians feared him until they experienced the reality of his transformation.

Transformation

Saul was on his way to Damascus to take prisoners there and bring them back to Jerusalem when nearing Damascus, a bright light shone all around him. "He fell to the ground and heard a voice say to him, 'Saul, Saul, why do you persecute me?'

'Who are you, Lord?' Saul asked. 'I am Jesus, whom you are persecuting,' he replied, 'Now get up and go into the city, and you will be told what you must do'" (Acts 9:4–6). At this point, Saul was blind and had to be led to Damascus by his associates. Jesus sent a disciple named Ananias, who lived in Damascus, to heal Saul. Thus began a new direction and a transformed life, one who became perhaps the greatest expositor of the Gospel of all time. During the first 13 chapters of Acts, he was known by

3. Dr. Walter A. Elwell and Dr. Philip W. Comfort, Editors, *Tyndale Bible Dictionary*, Wheaton, IL: Tyndale House Publishers, 2001, 513.

his given name, Saul; later he used the Roman name Paul throughout all of his writings.

In one of his epistles to his associate, Timothy, he gives a poignant statement of his gratitude for the grace of God toward him: "I thank Christ Jesus our Lord, who has given me strength, that he considered me faithful, appointing me to his service. Even though I was once a blasphemer and a persecutor and a violent man, I was shown mercy because I acted in ignorance and unbelief. The grace of our Lord was poured out on me abundantly, along with the faith and love that are in Christ Jesus. Here is a trustworthy saying that deserves full acceptance: Christ Jesus came into the world to save sinners—of whom I am the worst. But for that very reason I was shown mercy so that in me, the worst of sinners, Christ Jesus might display his unlimited patience as an example for those who would believe on him and receive eternal life" (1 Timothy 1:12–16). I include this lengthy comment here to illustrate that God is incredibly merciful. If he can forgive one who has committed such heinous deeds, he will forgive anyone who comes to him in genuine repentance.

His Ministry

As stated by Barker, Lane, and Ramsey, "By the end of the first century, the church was almost wholly Gentile in character. The most important bearer of the gospel to the Gentiles was the missionary-apostle Paul. Along with other companions, he embarked on three lengthy mission trips that took him as far as Rome. By the time of his death, every major church center in Asia and Europe had either been established through his labors or had some contact with his leadership. He made the letter an important vehicle for pastoral supervision and care. Thirteen of the twenty seven books of the New Testament are actually letters Paul addressed to churches and individuals."[4] These letters were widely circulated among the churches and eventually became part of the Christian canon, or Bible.

His epistle to the Romans is one of the most logical and intellectual examples of the reasoning behind the gospel. His letters in the New Testament are extensively employed in churches, Bible study groups, and Sunday school classes to teach doctrine and practical directions for living the Christian life. Through these vehicles, this man whose early career

---

4. Dr. Glenn Barker, Dr. William L. Lane, and Dr. J. Ramsey Michaels, Editors, *The New Testament Speaks*, New York: Harper and Row, 1969,143.

was dedicated to wiping out Christianity became its greatest champion. The tremendous zeal Paul once had for destroying the church of Jesus Christ had now turned around 180 degrees to being one of the foremost, if not the foremost, advocates of Jesus Christ. Now he fervently beseeches his fellow brothers and sisters in Christ to be strong in their faith. He educates them in all the nuances of their new faith, and he logically points out errors that were creeping into some of the individual young churches' practices. Each letter starts out lovingly with a greeting that includes terms of endearment, such as this one from 1 Timothy 1:2, "Grace, mercy, and peace from God the Father and Christ Jesus our Lord." Some of the letters follow with an expression of how Paul has thanked God for this body of believers, and how he has prayed for them. Typically, he goes into extensive details on the foundations of the Gospel, and then goes on to give the readers advice on the practicalities of Christian living. His passionate love permeates every epistle.

Hardships and Suffering

Paul's ministry was not an easy one. His life was filled with hardships and suffering he was very willing to endure. Throughout his ministry, detailed in the book of Acts and his 13 epistles, we encounter many incidents where Paul experiences horrible bodily harm. At times he was near death. Rather than detail many of these incidents individually, I have chosen a section of the book of Second Corinthians where Paul, in a poignant moment, details some of his harrowing experiences after criticism from false apostles: "I have worked much harder, been in prison more frequently, been flogged more severely, and been exposed to death again and again. Five times I received from the Jews the forty lashes minus one. Three times I was beaten with rods, once I was stoned, three times I was shipwrecked, I spent a night and a day in the open sea, I have been constantly on the move. I have been in danger from rivers, in danger from bandits, in danger from my own countrymen, in danger from Gentiles, in danger in the city, in danger in the country, in danger at sea; and in danger from false brothers. I have labored and toiled and have often gone without sleep; I have known hunger and thirst and have often gone without food; I have been cold and naked. Besides everything else, I face daily the pressure of my concern for all the churches" (2 Corinthians 11:23–28). If this were a job description, who among us would apply for this job? Many hearty souls would have given up their ministry after merely a few of the sufferings that Paul endured. Incredibly, he persevered, and we are all the richer for his perseverance. Finally, this man, once a vile persecutor and then a loving servant of Jesus Christ, enduring the most extreme suffering and hardships, can only be explained by the power of the Holy Spirit in his life. Such is the evidence of the reality of the Gospel of Jesus Christ.

9

Transformed Lives—Modern Times

*For it is God who works in you to will and to act
according to his good purpose.*

Philippians 2:13

*I will put my laws in their minds and write them on their hearts.
I will be their God, and they will be my people.*

Hebrews 8:10

IN MODERN TIMES, THE choices for selecting examples are unlimited. I could have selected from huge numbers of athletes, politicians, Hollywood stars, and the like. I chose several fascinating stories of individuals with spectacular, albeit unlikely, changes of direction. Charles "Chuck" Colson had a reputation as a hard-nosed political aide who would do almost anything to further the cause of President Nixon. After his conversion and being unfairly sentenced to prison, Colson became a new person. He now heads up a major prison ministry that has an outstanding record of presenting the Gospel to prisoners, helping them with their lives, and caring for their families. Moishe Rosen was a successful salesman and a secular Jew who had little religious inclination until his wife embraced Christianity. He eventually accepted Christ as his Savior and went on to run one of the most successful ministries ever, *Jews for Jesus*. Rabbi Moshe Laurie was anything but Rabbi material as an agent for Mossad, the Israeli intelligence agency. He often rejected Christians who came to his door when he was living in the United States. His story of conversion is an exciting one, and he now pastors a church in the Groton, Connecticut area.

THE HATCHET MAN—CHARLES "CHUCK" COLSON[1]

A Difficult Early Life

Life was not easy for young Charles W. Colson. Born during the depression years, his family experienced many hardships. His father had to drop out of high school as a teenager to support his widowed mother and his sister. After Chuck's father married, he spent twelve years in night school studying accounting and then law, all the while working days as a bookkeeper in a meat-packing plant. Chuck was born in 1931 and grew up in the Boston area. His father was in poor health and struggled to make a go of his law business. The family was heavily in debt. Chuck's father instilled in him a solid work ethic, and his parents made great sacrifices so Chuck could have a good education. He did not have much of a church or religious background. He attended Sunday school as a boy. He believed in God, and he occasionally prayed, but later had little religious activity in his life.

A solid student, Chuck was valedictorian of his class, served as editor of the school newspaper, and was voted most likely to succeed. Offered a "full ride" scholarship by Harvard, incredibly, Colson turned it down. He opted instead for a full Navy ROTC scholarship at Brown University. He was married the day he graduated from college and later fathered three children. In 1954, he became a platoon commander in the Marines. After his Marine stint, he worked days as he pursued a law degree nights at George Washington University.

A Career in Politics

Early in his career, he began to work in politics, and we learn of his opinion of "Boston-style" political activities: "I learned all the tricks, some of which went up to and even slightly over the legal boundaries. Phony mailings, tearing down opposition signs, planting misleading stories in the press, voting tombstones, and spying out the opposition in every possible way were all standard fare."[2] Colson eventually started his own law firm with a close friend. The business struggled with debt, but eventually stabilized. However, his preoccupation with politics and business took its toll

---

1. Charles W. Colson, *Born Again*. Fairfax, VA: Chosen Books, Inc., 1976.
2. Ibid., 27.

on his marriage. In January 1964 he was divorced. Later that year, he was remarried to Patty Hughes, who remains his wife to the present time.

A very close relationship developed with Richard Nixon that was to have great impact on Colson's life for many years. He met Nixon when the latter was Vice-President during the Eisenhower administration. Colson was impressed with Nixon's capabilities and vision for the country and his party. In 1964, he talked Nixon into running against Goldwater, albeit unsuccessfully. He then worked hard to get Nixon elected president in 1968. In 1969, Nixon brought Chuck onto his staff. Almost immediately, he was immersed into political imbroglios. With a penchant for getting "impossible" tasks accomplished, he became Nixon's "go-to guy." He became Nixon's Special Counsel. "But that same drive—getting the job done for the President whatever the cost—earned me the dubious title of Nixon's 'hatchet man.'"[3]

Watergate

In June of 1972, a burglary was reported at the Democratic National Headquarters in the Watergate complex. Although Colson had nothing to do with this crime, it had a major impact on his life to the present day. At the time, things seemed to be going very well for the Nixon administration. The economy was doing well, as was foreign policy. Nixon's political opponent, George McGovern, was having a hard time. Nixon's election by a large margin seemed a certainty. Without any basis in fact, the media began a massive attack on Colson. Although he had nothing to do with Watergate, his history as a reputed "hatchet man" resulted in many persons in the media and government assuming his involvement.

Tom Phillips' Testimony

The election went as expected, Nixon coasting with an immense margin. Colson went back to his law offices and had many clients lined up. One of these important clients was the Raytheon Company, the largest employer in New England. After a set of all-day meetings at Raytheon, Tom Phillips, the company president, requested a meeting with Colson. As he was heading to the meeting, an executive from Raytheon informed him that Phillips had changed since Chuck had last seen him—it was some kind of religious experience. Chuck noticed a difference in Tom's demeanor. He

3. Ibid., 57.

seemed very serene, whereas in the past, his activities had been very intense. After a period of discussing various subjects, Chuck mentioned that he had heard Tom was involved in religious activities. Tom replied, "Yes, that's true Chuck. I have accepted Jesus Christ. I have committed my life to him and it has been the most marvelous experience of my whole life." Chuck did not reply to Tom, but in his own words, "But he had struck a raw nerve—the empty life. It was what I was living with, though I couldn't admit that to Tom. I went back to Washington to struggle with my inner malaise—and Watergate— and Phillip's astonishing words."[4]

Second-hand claims by a few of those associated with the Nixon administration made Colson a repeated target throughout the media. At his lawyer's suggestion, he took the first of a series of lie detector tests. Richard Arthur, a man with impressive qualifications, administered the test.[5] After extensive testing, including many negative activities from Chuck's background to establish a sound baseline for the test, Chuck awaited the results of the investigation. David Shapiro, his attorney, was later able to break the news: "You passed—flying colors. No doubt that you are telling the truth." The New York Times reported the successful test. However, even the Times and the Washington Post generated articles over following weeks that cast questions on the findings.[6] Government investigations of various aspects of the Nixon administration continued, accompanied by a barrage of newspaper headlines and articles that were filled with innuendos implicating Colson.

Chuck was under enormous pressures. His introspections raised questions about himself, his purpose, and what his life was all about. He thought about his meeting with Tom Phillips, and how Phillips had become such a caring, serene, person. With a visit to the Boston area planned, Chuck called Phillips and they scheduled a meeting at Tom's home.

Tom told Chuck about how he came to be Raytheon's president at age 40—all of the drive and hard work. He told how he was very successful but felt a terrible emptiness.

He began to read the Scriptures and search for direction. While on business in New York, he noticed that Billy Graham was having a crusade

4. Ibid., 93.
5. Ibid., 96.
6. Ibid., 99.

in Madison Square Garden. He decided to attend, and he turned his life over to Jesus Christ at the crusade.

Chuck was surprised that it was as easy as just accepting Jesus as Savior. Tom continued to relate how his life changed and how he was so excited about his new way of life. They also discussed the negative activities among so many persons in the Nixon administration and how destructive those actions were. At first, Chuck was defensive, but gradually, as they continued their discussion, he began to see that Tom was right. Eventually, Tom challenged Chuck to make the decision to accept Christ. Tom did not pressure Chuck. Rather, he gave Chuck a copy of C.S. Lewis's book, *Mere Christianity*,[7] and they prayed together. As he was outside the home, Chuck regretted not making the decision for Christ, but it was too late to go back. He sat in the car weeping, and he prayed.

Transformation

He and Patty embarked on a vacation in Maine. It allowed Chuck to ponder all of the situations swirling about his life: slams in the media, prosecutors who were looking for any excuse to indict him, and the spiritual facts to which he was being exposed. He read *Mere Christianity* and continued to search for the truth that would govern the future direction of his life. One morning, toward the end of the week in Maine, he describes the culmination of all his reflections: "And so early that Friday morning, while I sat alone staring at the sea I love, words I had not been certain I could understand or say fell naturally from my lips: 'Lord Jesus, I believe you. I accept you. Please come into my life. I commit it to you.'"[8]

Trial and Incarceration

Two years after the break-in, Colson was urged to accept a plea bargain. Although he maintained his innocence in this particular matter, the plea bargain would eliminate a trial, bring closure to the proceedings, and prevent the possibility of a much tougher sentence. However, to accept the plea bargain, he would have to agree that he was involved in the Watergate activities, which he was not. In other words, he would have to lie. Now, as a Christian, he was unwilling to lie. Meanwhile, he passed his second

7. C. S. Lewis, *Mere Christianity*, New York: Macmillan Publishing Co.,1960.
8. Ibid., Colson, 130.

and third lie detector tests easily. Although the prosecutor's office knew of these results, Colson was indicted.

The judges had made prior biased public statements, but they refused to disqualify themselves or to change the venue. Chuck decided to plead guilty to disseminating derogatory information to the press about Daniel Ellsberg while Ellsberg was a criminal defendant. Ironically, this was not a crime! However, he was sentenced to 1 to 3 years in prison and a $5,000 fine. Others who committed serious crimes received lesser sentences. This is the story of a man who, against his attorney's advice, pled guilty to an action that is not a crime. He could have plea-bargained, but he chose not to do so. Why? Because his life had been transformed by the Lord. Although the action he took against Daniel Ellsberg was not a crime, Colson knew it was wrong. This was his way of atoning for a prior dirty trick.

How do we know that a person like Colson had a transformed life? It is often suspected that someone who is enmeshed in a circumstance leading to incarceration conveniently "finds religion." It is assumed the person is looking for favored treatment. Chuck was so accused in many articles in the media. However, the evidence of his transformation was dramatic. Once he accepted Christ as Savior, all of his behavior changed. He confronted former enemies and apologized. He asked for forgiveness. Even Democrats who were Christians came beside Chuck and became supporters. That would not happen if he were merely acting out a role.

Prison life was all that one might fear it could be. Everything was designed to dehumanize the person, including the depressing clothing that was issued. Reasons to fear were everywhere. During the whole period of the sentence, Chuck was under the cloud of a rumor that someone was going to kill him. He did not know who it could be. Day in, day out, he had to be watchful. Even in this environment, he had the persistence to live as he felt that a Christian should. He developed a group of believers. Some had fallen away from their walk with the Lord, which is how they got into prison. They held Bible studies and prayer gatherings, and they supported one another. The group grew dynamically in numbers and commitment to God.

After some time in prison, Chuck was confronted in a secluded area by two men, one of whom was a former police lieutenant who believed that his arrest and conviction was caused by an investigation he attributed to Chuck while still in the Nixon administration. Although it was not stated at the time, this man was likely the one who had threatened Colson's life.

After a lengthy and heated discussion, the man relented. Chuck explained the investigation was not initiated by the administration but by the Justice Department. The man believed Chuck because of his reputation for honesty gained throughout his prison term.

Return to "Ordinary" Life

Chuck was released, and he could have returned to a successful law practice for personal gain. He did not. How he comported himself once he was released is evidence for the reality of his experience with Jesus Christ. The following items were obtained from the website of Prison Fellowship Ministries, the organization initiated and developed by Chuck:[9]

> Colson's heart is ever with the prisoner. He has clearly never forgotten the promise he made to his fellow inmates during his brief stay in prison: that he would "never forget those behind bars."
> In 1976, Colson founded Prison Fellowship Ministries, which, in collaboration with churches of all confessions and denominations, has become the world's largest outreach to prisoners, ex-prisoners, crime victims, and their families. Colson has spent the last 25 years as head of Prison Fellowship Ministries.
>
> Colson has visited prisons throughout the U.S. and the world and has built a movement working with more than 40,000 prison ministry volunteers, with ministries in 100 countries. In the course of touring prisons worldwide, he became deeply concerned with prison conditions and the need for better access to religious programs.
>
> To help stem the cycle of crime and poverty, Prison Fellowship, under Colson's leadership, introduced Angel Tree, a program that provides Christmas presents to more than 500,000 children of inmates annually on behalf of their incarcerated parents, These simple acts of kindness have revitalized hope and reconciliation among millions of children and their families, many of whom subsist below the poverty level.
>
> While Colson is one of the Christian community's most sought-after speakers, he has resolutely refused to establish a speaking fee. Perhaps anticipating criticism of any appearance of self-enrichment by a former Watergate figure, Colson donates all speaking honoraria and book royalties to Prison Fellowship, and accepts the salary of a mid-range ministry executive.

9. Prison Fellowship Ministries website, www.pfm.org., 2004. Used by permission from Prison Fellowship Ministries.

In recognition of his work, Colson received the prestigious Templeton Prize for Progress in Religion in 1993, donating the $1 million prize to Prison Fellowship. Colson's other awards have included the Humanitarian Award, Dominos Pizza Corporation (1991) and The Others Award, The Salvation Army (1990).

JEWS FOR JESUS—FOUNDER: MOISHE ROSEN[10]

Moishe Rosen is one of the most fascinating persons I have ever met. Over the years, he has spoken at my church, Peninsula Covenant Church in Redwood City, California, many times. Our church is geographically close to Jews for Jesus, and many of our church attendees support the ministry. I have always enjoyed his sermons—filled with interesting information on the history of Jews for Jesus and on the importance of Jews finding their Messiah, Jesus Christ. He speaks with great authority, intelligence, and a wonderful folksy humor; and yet, it was not always this way for Moishe. But for a couple of forks in the road where the right decisions were made, Moishe would have been a great salesman in Colorado, not a Christian, and Jews for Jesus would not have come into being.

Early Life

Moishe was born Martin Meyer Rosen in Kansas City, Missouri on April 12, 1932 into a family that observed many, but not all, of the tenets of Orthodox Judaism. He was given the name Moishe at his circumcision. The Rosens later moved to Denver, Colorado, where Moishe learned early in life, as an elementary school student, Jews were different. At Christmas time, he came home from singing carols at school only to find out from his mother that carols were not for Jews. He also encountered anti-Semitism early from children near his home, who treated him badly because he was a Jew.

Although Moishe attended Hebrew school, there was not a lot of religious influence in the home. In fact, his father often said that "religion is a racket."[11] He also learned a serious work ethic from his hard-working father and was involved in chores at a very young age in the family scrap-iron business. At age 15, he lied about his age and joined the

---

10. Moishe Rosen, *Jews for Jesus*, Old Tappan, NJ: Fleming H. Revell Co., 1974; Dr. Ruth A. Tucker, *Not Ashamed*, Sisters, OR: Multnomah Publishers, 1999; and Ruth Rosen, *Testimonies of Jews Who Believe in Jesus*, San Francisco: Purple Pomegranate Productions, 1992.

11. Ibid., M. Rosen, 17.

National Guard. His unit was activated in the late 1940s because of a crisis with the Soviet Union in Berlin.[12] Even there he encountered a blatantly anti-Semitic first sergeant, who made obscene comments about Moishe's mother. Eventually, Moishe reacted by hitting the sergeant in the head with his carbine.

When he made his first foray into a search for employment, a personnel director told him he was qualified for the job, but the company did not hire Jews. Since Moishe thought the world consisted of Jews and other folks who were Christians, needless to say, he did not have a high opinion of Christians. Of course, at that time, he had no idea that many persons who called themselves Christians did not follow the commandments of Jesus Christ. It is amazing that Moishe later became a Christian, when he had experienced so many evil inputs from so-called Christians. In Moishe's own words, "In those days I really believed that if you scratched a Gentile, or a 'Christian,' you'd find an anti-Semite. I was a Jew, militantly protective of my heritage."[13] However, we have also seen in chapter five that God often selects persons to serve him who are very unlikely candidates! It is to Moishe's credit that he eventually understood God's plan and responded accordingly.

Ceil's Journey

The spiritual journey of Moishe's wife Ceil was a huge turning point in her life and eventually in that of Moishe's. Ceil was raised by foster parents in an Orthodox Jewish home near Boston. The laws of orthodoxy were strictly observed. One of Ceil's early observations tells us something about where she was spiritually: "I didn't really love God: nobody had ever told me I should. I only knew that I was supposed to obey Him."[14] When she was 13 years old, the family moved to Denver. It was a time when Ceil began to question the tenets of her Orthodox upbringing. She even began questioning God's existence. When she was 16, Ceil participated in her high school Christmas pageant. Singing the Christmas song, "Oh come, oh come Immanuel, and ransom captive Israel," stirred her thinking about Jesus. She realized that he was Jewish, and wondered if he was the Messiah, but did not make any major changes to her beliefs at that time.

12. Ibid., 19.

13. Ibid.

14. Ibid., R. Rosen, 3.

Marriage to Ceil

The best thing that happened to Moishe, besides later becoming a Christian, occurred during one of his jobs as a teenager. One day, at the age of 14, Moishe was at the front door, selling door numbers. He did not make a sale, but he was impressed with the pretty young resident. He asked her for a date, but Ceil was too shy to accept. As a result of his persistence, a year later they went for a walk and then began to go steady.[15] Moishe and Ceil were married at age 18, and decided not to keep an Orthodox home, a happy decision for Ceil. At this point in her life, Ceil was a professed atheist, and Moishe kept some of the holiday observances for cultural reasons, but that was the extent of his involvement. There they were, Ceil an atheist and Moishe perhaps agnostic at best. How unlikely it was that they would come to a belief in Jesus Christ. How unlikely that these two would be the human implements of the Holy Spirit in developing one of the most successful mission endeavors in the world.

Spiritual Stirrings

A year after marriage, they were expecting their first child. Ceil was so happy, she began to say prayers of thanksgiving to God. She was not sure what to believe about God, but she did come to believe he was "at the controls."[16] The next major effect on Ceil's beliefs took place when they went to see *Quo Vadis*. They did not go for any religious reason. Rather, it was to see an epic film in color, special in those days. However, the film did make an impact on Ceil. Later, Moishe bought her an album of Christmas songs, because he knew she enjoyed them for the music, but not for religious reasons. However, she was deeply moved by the song, *O Little Town of Bethlehem.*

She began to pray for God's guidance in what she should believe. She began to think about reading the New Testament, but was afraid because of reactions from her family. Eventually, she talked a cousin into buying a Bible for her, and she started to read the Gospels. She declared, "It's hard to describe what I found so irresistible about Jesus. First of all, it was obvious that he was Jewish." Additionally, she thought, "He was so practical, down-to-earth, I guess you could say—and at the same time, there was something unmistakably divine about him. He spoke with authority. He was compas-

15. Ibid., 3.
16. Ibid., 4.

sionate, yet inspired respect and his commands were a call to righteousness. As I read, I knew he was not just a mystery hero. He was real."[17]

Ceil longed to discuss her thoughts with someone, but did not know how to go about it. Again, she prayed for God's direction. His answer came in dramatic fashion. A missionary, Mrs. Hannah Wago, knocked on her door. A Christian family had been praying for the Rosens for years, totally unaware of Ceil's spiritual journey, and asked Mrs. Wago to visit them. The two ladies embarked on a weekly Bible study, much of it from the prophets. In Ceil's words, "I soaked up the Bible like a sponge."[18] Then, the inevitable happened. Moishe knew about her Bible readings, and he began to worry. One day, when she was on the phone with Mrs. Wago, Moishe came home and was so angry, he tore the phone from the wall. Later, when he confronted her about her beliefs, she beseeched him not to make her choose between him and God. She would choose Moishe in any other situation. Moishe's love for her was so great, that he did not take any other precipitous actions.

Jesus, Their Messiah

With Moishe's knowledge, she went to church with Mrs. Wago on Easter Sunday in 1953. At the end of the service, the minister gave an invitation to those who would like to accept Jesus as Savior. Ceil went forward. She then began to pray fervently for her husband. Moishe began reading with the idea of refuting Christianity, but as many experienced before him, such readings often lead to accepting Christianity as the truth. Both he and Ceil were surprised when Moishe "confessed his faith" to her and then asked, "Now what do I do?" They prayed together for him to accept Jesus as his Messiah. The next day, they went to church and Moishe went forward at the minister's invitation.[19]

With no experience as to Christian services, jargon, traditions, etc., Moishe and Ceil had a lot to learn, but learn they did. They were very conscientious in pursuing their new belief system. The really hard part was breaking the news to their parents. Moishe's father told him to get out of the house. Ceil's parents reacted even more harshly. They requested that Moishe and Ceil meet with a Rabbi, which they did. Ceil's parents were

17. Ibid., 5–6.
18. Ibid., 7.
19. Ibid., 9.

with them. Moishe and Ceil quoted passages from Isaiah 53 and Jeremiah 31 from the Hebrew Bible. The Rabbi was unable to respond, disappointing Ceil's parents. Unfortunately, they still rejected Ceil. They eventually left town, and the Rosens never heard from them again.[20]

Moishe adopted Christianity with an enormous zeal. He firmly believed God clearly wanted him to devote his life to telling other Jews about Jesus.[21] However, Moishe knew he needed to know more about the Bible and Christianity to be proficient in ministry, so he decided to attend Bible college. When he told his family about his decision to go to Northeastern Bible College, his father suggested that Moishe needed to go to a psychiatrist. While many persons might be insulted at such a suggestion, Moishe respectfully went to the doctor. After two sessions, he received a letter from the psychiatrist informing him that he was normal. With his typical wry humor, Moishe said, "So no matter what anyone says about my mental stability these days, I at least have a letter to prove my sanity. Most people don't."[22]

A New Ministry is Born

Upon his graduation, Moishe began serving with the American Board of Missions to the Jews, and was assigned to head up the work in Los Angeles. After arriving in California, he soon experienced feelings of inadequacy. "My main problem on our arrival in California was finding a point at which to start. My objective was to establish a foothold for Jewish evangelism, and in effect I had to start from scratch."[23] The Lord blessed the fledgling ministry by bringing many Jewish seekers to the mission services. Moishe became proficient in discussing the Gospel to all kinds of Jewish people.

"But perhaps the greatest challenge I faced was trying to preach effectively to hostile street crowds."[24] He started learning how to conduct street preaching sessions while still in college, but it took a while before he felt comfortable with it. With his characteristic persistence, he mastered reaching Jews through public meetings.

20. Ibid., 10.
21. Ibid., Tucker, 28.
22. Ibid., M. Rosen, 36.
23. Ibid., 39.
24. Ibid., 40.

His success in Los Angeles did not go unnoticed. He was given a promotion and was moved back to New York City to organize a training program for candidates in Jewish missions. Moishe developed an excellent program; however, he felt that the manifold requirements of the organization were interfering with how he perceived his mission to reach Jews for Jesus. As was his custom, he prayed to God for direction, and God did not fail him. Through a friend, Moishe was challenged to reach out to hippies. It was pointed out to him that many hippies are Jewish. Moishe took the criticism to heart, and the first step toward establishing Jews for Jesus was taken. The sixties were the height of the hippie movement and they were easy to find in New York. At the recommendation of another friend, he went to Greenwich Village and began interacting, so he could learn how to relate to them. He needed to be creative, as the conventional forms of Gospel communications were not effective. He came up with one new format on a single sheet of paper with a drawing and effective short comments that inspired questions. This tract was the first of a new genre of literature, later called "Broadsides," that has been one of the major forms of communication of Jews for Jesus.[25]

Increasingly, Moishe felt that God was leading him back to a work with street people in California. After conversations with Dr. Fuchs, the head of the American Board of Missions to the Jews, Moishe resigned his position with the organization. Once again he headed west with his family and some female workers. Gradually, he began to build an organization with young Jews who had accepted Jesus as the Messiah, and Jews for Jesus was born in 1970. There was no model for this type of work, so Moishe had to develop the principles by which this ministry would succeed.

Principles and Methods

Moishe was very concerned about the poor results other organizations had in trying to reach Jews. As described by Tucker, "Most of the missions were continuing to do the things they had always done with minimal success and without realizing that programs once established to speak to a particular situation were hanging limply in place long after the situation had changed."[26] Tucker continues: "The problem, according to Moishe, was 'how to communicate to people who did not want to hear our message

25. Ibid., 60.
26. Ibid., Tucker, 31.

and were sure that they already knew why anything we would tell them about Jesus couldn't be true.' How to communicate has been Moishe's vision ever since. For more than twenty-five years communication has been the driving force for Moishe—and for Jews for Jesus." The idea is to present the good news the way Jesus himself might present it—with love and compassion—and let others decide whether they will be insulted or intrigued.[27] An important strategy has been to confront people on streets, in parks, or wherever the target audience is, encouraging individual encounters and discussion.

Who the Jews for Jesus are is often confusing to people, especially non-Christian Jews. Many claim that the believers are no longer Jews. However, being a Jew is significantly different than belonging to other religions or ethnic groups. If one is a Christian, Muslim, or a member of another religious organization, he no longer is one if he recants his beliefs. One does not cease to be a Jew if he embraces another religion. His or her "Jewishness" goes beyond the belief system. According to Jewish law, a person is a Jew if his mother is Jewish, or if he converts to Judaism.[28] If a person has a Jewish mother and becomes an atheist, he or she is still a Jew. Moishe Rosen is a Baptist minister, but he is still a Jew and proud of it.

An important principle of the movement is for workers to be involved in their communities: "We Jews for Jesus, then, are a tribe of contrasting individuals who have been welded together by one primary goal: We want to let nonbelievers, and especially young Jews, know what Jesus has done for us. We are not, however, a separate, isolated sect. Most of us also belong to nearby churches, where we serve on committees, teach Sunday-school classes, and participate in musical programs."[29] Undoubtedly, the most important principle guiding the organization is dependence on the Holy Spirit for direction. The ministry emphasizes Bible study and prayer to aid in personal development and for guidance in all decisions.

Other characteristics of the movement are high standards in all they do, and creativity in their methods. They have come up with many techniques to fit the particular needs of the target audience. The broadsides that have been mentioned previously, have been incredibly successful. My wife and I looked forward to receiving them at Forty-Niner

27. Ibid., 10.
28. Ibid., M. Rosen, 95.
29. Ibid., 85.

games, because they were so innovative, humorous, and made one think. We enjoyed greeting the workers with a Shalom and letting them know how much we appreciated their efforts. The music group, "The Liberated Wailing Wall," is world renowned for their great singing, meaningful content, and Jewish-oriented melodies. The organization has been successful with drama groups, street preaching, and one-on-one discussions. However, they are always adaptable. Methods are always under review for continuing effectiveness.

Opposition

Jews for Jesus has undoubtedly received more opposition than any other missions organization. It is rare for Gentile missionaries to be scorned by families or members of Christian organizations. Jews who become Christians are often shunned or disowned by family and friends. Jews for Jesus frequently encounter hostility at their street programs. Hecklers try to disrupt the speakers or performers. However, the workers have been taught by Moishe to accept the heckling with humor and good nature, often turning those encounters to their own advantage. A number of hecklers who persistently came to street meetings eventually became Christians! Why? Because while heckling, they were hearing the word of God, and it eventually sank in.

Blessed with Success

How does one measure success? For Jews for Jesus, it would primarily be measured by how well did it communicate its message, and how did its target audience respond? There is no question that Jews for Jesus has been outstanding in reaching people for Jesus Christ, "first for the Jew, then for the Gentile," as first stated by the apostle Paul in Romans 1:16. Communications methods have always been creative and effective, adapted over the years as the needs of the target audience changed. Huge numbers of Jews have embraced their Messiah, and even greater numbers of Gentiles have done so.

Jews for Jesus has grown over the years into the largest and most visible of the Messianic Jewish organizations.[30] "Today Moishe is regarded by many as the twentieth century's leading missiologist in the field of Jewish evangelism." Jews for Jesus moved from the confines of the United States

30. Ibid., Tucker, 35.

to other countries, although it was never a strategy to develop a world-wide ministry. The movement to other countries came about as needs were perceived, typically where there were large concentrations of Jews. The first overseas branch was initiated in South Africa in 1989, accompanied by extreme opposition from the Jewish establishment. Appearances by The Liberated Wailing Wall and the New Jerusalem Players had to be canceled. Yet the persistence of the committed Jews for Jesus workers paid off with an ongoing ministry there. "In almost every instance where Jews for Jesus has opened new areas of ministry, The Liberated Wailing Wall has been actively involved."[31] However, opposition was also omnipresent. In London, an office was opened in 1991, and the British press was highly critical. Vandals continuously caused damage to the facility, and tore down posters. Undaunted, the United Kingdom ministry has thrived, and Jews for Jesus has continued to expand overseas as the Lord has inspired and where he has laid the need upon the hearts of dedicated staff members. In addition to South Africa and London, outposts have been established in Paris, Tel Aviv, Sydney, Buenos Aires, Toronto, Essen, Odessa, Moscow, and other cities of the former Soviet Union.

A New Direction

In 1996, Moishe gave up the reins of the organization he had nursed along since its inception. He was 64 years of age. He felt that it was for the good of the movement that he step aside for younger leadership. As was typical of his style, he did not choose his successor. That was a task for the council as led by the Holy Spirit. After a day of prayer and fasting, they went through numerous votes, until a unanimous decision was reached. The "mantle" was passed to David Brickner, then 37 years old. After the unanimous vote, all gathered joyfully around David to commission him for the great task before him.[32]

Of course, this was also a new direction for Moishe, but not retirement. He still works with Jews for Jesus, and is active in a number of areas. He now has time for individual contacts, always one of his great strengths. He also spends time on his computer, ministering to people all over the world. One of his favorite activities is engaging others in spiritual discus-

31. Ibid., 187.
32. Ibid., 249.

sions in chat rooms. He also continues to speak in Christian churches and other venues.

Here again is an example of a transformed life. What a great ministry he has had and continues to have. As stated earlier, how different it might have been if certain threads within his life were different. What if Ceil never became interested in the possibility that Jesus could be the Messiah? What if Moishe continued to resist the witness of the Lord in Ceil's life and the call of the Lord for Moishe to accept him? But we do not need to conjecture upon these possibilities. Moishe and Ceil were obedient to their Messiah, and one of the great missions movements became a reality and is still thriving—a tribute to their obedience, and evidence of the working of the Holy Spirit in mighty ways.

FROM "SPOOK" TO JESUS—RABBI MOSHE LAURIE[33]

Israeli Defender

Moshe Laurie was born an Orthodox Jew in Brooklyn, NY. In his own words, he was always looking for the Messiah since he was 9 years old. His grandparents were killed in Warsaw during the Nazi occupation in Europe in World War II. At 9 1/2 years old he made the decision that such an atrocity would not happen again. "I was going to be a guardian of Israel. He joined the U.S. Marines at 17 years of age, and volunteered for all the combat schools in preparation for serving Israel. He went to Israel and became a member of the Israeli National Police. He was involved in developing a sniper program for airports. Eventually, he moved over to the defense forces as the assistant commander of the sniper school training and antiterrorist program.

The Spiritual Journey

Moshe was not open to the witness of Christians. Before he became a Christian, he traveled a lot and was often visited by Christians knocking on the door. He immediately told them that he was Jewish. Some were still persistent in telling him that he needed to hear about the Messiah, Jesus. He again told them, "I'm Jewish. Leave me alone. I have enough problems."

33. Interview with Dr. D. James Kennedy, *Rabbi Laurie*, Ft. Lauderdale, FL: Coral Ridge Ministries videotape, PGM #0450, December 12, 2004. Used by permission from Coral Ridge Ministries.

Still some politely persisted. Moshe's way of dealing with that situation was "to spit on him and close the door." So, as the narrator states it, "How did a nice middle-aged Jewish boy like Moshe Laurie come to believe that Jesus was the Christ, the Messiah?"

It began when he traveled back to the United States in 1982, and settled in Las Cruces, New Mexico. He had decided to take a break from his work with the Mossad in Israel. In his Coral Ridge interview, it was clear he was not going to describe his activities with this organization, but this agency is responsible for intelligence collection, covert action (including paramilitary activities and assassinations), and counter-terrorism. Mossad is one of the world's most well-known intelligence agencies, and is often viewed in the same regard as the CIA and the British MI6.

In Las Cruces, Moshe was making extra money on the side by doing a little camera work with a video camcorder. He learned of an upcoming sports awards dinner, and he was invited to come and tape the event. Then, he found out the awards dinner was being held by the sponsor of the league, the largest Catholic church in Las Cruces. Reflecting on the situation at that time, "I didn't go to Catholic churches because I was told since childhood that the Devil lives there, so I didn't go." But he had already been paid, and he had no intention of paying it back. So, he told the priest he was coming, but to do the awards first, because, "If you start waving smoke, I am out of there." However, what happened next was totally unexpected. The awards dinner started, and he was videotaping when he suddenly heard a voice saying, "You can serve the Father through me. You will serve the Father through me, for I have come in his stead." Moshe started "to cry like a baby."

"Now here I am, the big security hot-shot. I don't trust anybody for anything. If this were not supernatural, I would have taken the camera apart to see who's playing with me. I knew at that moment that this was the Messiah, and I knew at that moment it was Jesus." Now that he had begun to have a faith in Jesus as Messiah, he had to rethink everything that he had believed for the first 39 years of his life. For 39 years, he had been a practicing Orthodox Jew, always seeking the Messiah.

He found the Assembly of God Church in Las Cruces. He walked in and announced, "I'm Jewish and I am saved. What do I do now?" An 80-year old man told him to sit down, and he did. The old man told him to read the New Testament. He read it in a very short time, and realized he is "the temple of the Holy Spirit." He believed the Word was absolute and exact,

"When I realized that the Messiah that I have been looking for has been here for 2,000 years; when I realized that I could have these gifts, I was like a little kid in a candy store. It's almost indescribable the joy and the happiness and the power of something that you sought all your life, and it scared the heck out of me when I realized that the Messiah was Jesus."

Rejection in Israel

This change in perspective would obviously prove to have great repercussions for this member of the Israeli security organization. With his multitude of passports, identification documents, and secret identities, he came "trotting back to Israel. I came through the door, absolutely nutty, going 'the Meshiach has come, the Messiah has come.'" He was married to an Israeli and had two children, and was still with the security services. Moshe continues, "So they decided that I was scripturally insane and that my wife must be saved from me. So they divorced me against my will and I left in 60 days." In Israel, a funeral was held and they "sat Shiva," a seven-day mourning period for him. They considered him dead, because he accepted a false Messiah.

Moshe returned to the United States and changed his name. He lived under the assumed name for seven years because he was afraid that they were going to kill him. After seven years, he decided to return to his original name. He attended a seminary and went into the ministry. As he tells it, "God used me in many different and crazy places. If someone would ask me today, did I ever think that I would ever be a believer in the Jewish Messiah Yeshua, whose name is Jesus, who is also the Christian Messiah—he's everyone's Messiah—would I ever believe that I would be a believer—not on this earth. I would probably laugh myself stupid and run you out."

In an amusing anecdote, Moshe recalls a question that he had from his early childhood about a passage in the first chapter of Genesis. In Genesis 1:26, it says, "Let us make man in our own image." As a little boy, Moshe went to the Rabbi and asked him who are "us." He said, "Sit down. When you are old enough, you will know." So, as Moshe relates it, "So I waited. I waited." When he was 13 years old, he said, "I'm a man supposedly. I went to the Rabbi and asked who are 'us?' How can it be plural, because Judaism preaches the one true God." He said, "If God wants to call himself 'Us,' who are we to question him?" "He didn't know either." When

Moshe became a believer, he started to read the Bible from the beginning. When he got to "Us," he knew what "Us" means. In his words, "Father, Son, and the Holy Spirit. 39 years old and I didn't know who 'Us' is. When I got to Isaiah, I almost got angry with my teachers. You could have shown me this." He was referring here to the clear prophecy, especially in Isaiah 53, that predicted centuries before, what would happen to Jesus.

Then, God gave Moshe a very difficult task. Moshe had balked at telling his 82-year old mother about his beliefs, but God gave him a clear directive to do so. As he states it, "No Jewish boy, I don't care if he is an adult, wants to tell his Mama something that she does not want to hear. But I came back after all the years to my Mama, and I walked in. She said to me, "What are you doing?" And Moshe said, "I'm teaching the Torah, and I am studying. My Mama turns to me and says to me, 'Any God who can bring my son from hunting people and other things and go back to study the Torah has to be the God." Moshe then said to her, "Mama, it's not just my God, it's your God." At that point, they prayed the sinners prayer together. She had accepted the Lord. Moshe continues, "She passed away three years later with a smile on her face, and I know that she is waiting for me."

Ministry

He also became reconciled to other members of his family. Two of his children, amazingly became believers independent of his influence, another example of how incredibly God works in people's lives. However, he had lost the wife of his youth, but God blessed him with another loving wife, a Godly woman who helps him with his ministries. Today, Rabbi Moshe Laurie pastors in the Groton, Connecticut area. His church, Shofar Be Tzion Ministries operates in tandem with the New Life Church, headed by Pastor Johnny Burns. He also directs "Bible Voice Broadcasting USA," and he became the first to broadcast into the Holy Land in Hebrew, which he does from his home. He also hosts two community cable TV shows. Similarly to Moishe Rosen and Jews for Jesus, he wants Christians to appreciate the Jewish roots of Christianity. Together with "High Adventure Gospel Communication Ministries" in Canada, and "Bible Voice UK," they are bringing the "voice of the Lord to the ends of the earth."[34]

---

34. Shofar Be Tzion Ministries website, www.shofarbetzion.com.

Moshe is just another example of the myriad of individuals who have found Jesus as their Messiah, and as with the others, amazing things happen as the Holy Spirit takes charge of a new direction in their transformed lives. As the Coral Ridge interview concluded, Moshe was able to express what the Messiah means to him: "Eight months after returning to the United States, a message came from Israel. They told me to come back and talk to some people. Renounce the Messiah. Tell them that you were under stress from work. Study with a Rabbi. All will be forgiven. Go back to your wife. Your family will be reinstated. You will get your job back (he was very good at what he did)." All he had to do was renounce the Messiah. "I would not do it, and I am glad that I didn't. I am on the greatest adventure of my life. I love the Lord unto death, and because I love him to death, I don't have to die. I would not trade him for anybody or anything on this earth."

As can be seen from all of the above cases, from New Testament times to the present, lives are transformed when Jesus Christ becomes one's Savior. I could have chosen from so many other persons in demonstrating these major changes in people's lives. However, the above cases serve as a small but significant sampling of myriads of cases. In my opinion, such transformations, as well as my own, are additional evidence of God's existence and the power of the Holy Spirit. Perhaps you know of such cases. I hope that you do. If so, talk to them to get additional insights into this wonderful way of life—and eventually, eternal life!

RECOMMENDED READING

Charles W Colson, *Born Again*. Fairfax, VA: Chosen Books, Inc, 1976.
Moishe Rosen, *Jews for Jesus*, Old Tappan, NJ: Fleming H. Revell Co., 1974.
Dr. Ruth A. Tucker, *Not Ashamed*, Sisters, OR: Multnomah Publishers, 1999.
Ruth Rosen, *Testimonies of Jews Who Believe in Jesus*, San Francisco: Purple Pomegranate Productions, 1992.

10

My Personal Experiences with God

The Lord is my light and my salvation—whom shall I fear?
The Lord is the strength of my life—of whom shall I be afraid?

Psalm 27:1

IN THE LAST FEW chapters, I have discussed the basics of Christianity and I have shown how lives have been transformed in amazing ways; first in the lives of the apostles, then in selected lives in modern times. The premise was that when an individual accepts Jesus Christ as one's Savior, great changes take place in the individual's life. We saw how the apostles were transformed from easily frightened people to very bold expositors of the gospel. The apostle Paul, who had been trying to stamp out Christianity, became its greatest proponent. Chuck Colson, Moishe Rosen, and Rabbi Laurie all became great leaders of Christian ministries.

At this point, I want to relate some selected experiences from my own life as further evidence of the working of the Holy Spirit in a Christian's life. After all, if the Gospel is true, should we not expect that God is involved in the lives of believers? Does it make sense that the Christian is on his or her own in coping with life's difficulties? Does not God bring about circumstances in the lives of his believers to bring about his purposes for those lives?

To illustrate instances of God's working in a Christian's life, I have selected just a few situations from my own life that I believe clearly show the reality of God bringing about his will. These are not all of the experiences I could present, but certain ones that are representative of how the Holy Spirit was involved at certain key points in my life. I also emphasize that my life is not constantly filled with such occurrences. There have been long periods during which I have not experienced such events. In his sovereignty, God chooses when his involvement is appropriate. I also emphasize that any one of these items could be challenged as a coincidence. However, I believe that taken as a body of evidence, it would take more faith to believe that they are coincidental than not.

SPINAL MENINGITIS

When I was in high school, I became very ill. My temperature rose to 104 degrees Fahrenheit. I remember calling out to my mother and telling her, "I have to think to breathe." I am sure my statement was just the delusion of a feverish mind, but it seemed real at the time. My mother called our family doctor. In those days, the doctor would come to the house if the illness was serious. He gave me an extensive examination, bending my body in various ways, checking the flexibility of my joints. As a result, I was diagnosed with spinal meningitis, a very serious malady at that time. Very few recovered.

I was rushed to the hospital and placed in the isolation ward, and my mother went home to pray. It was not unusual for Mom to be on her knees praying for long periods of time when there were special needs. I later learned from her that after an extensive time of prayer, she received an assurance from the Lord that I would be all right. At the same time, as near as I could place it later, my fever broke and all symptoms of meningitis were gone. I called in the nurse and asked her to call my mother to bring a radio to me so that I could listen to that night's baseball game. I felt fine! Was this a coincidence? I don't think so.

THE GIRL OF MY DREAMS

Except for my conversion to evangelical Christianity, the next best thing that ever happened to me was meeting June Motta. Prior to that wonderful event, I had wondered if I ever would meet the woman who would become my wife. I was twenty-five years old at the time, and most of my friends were married. All through college, the Air Force, and much of my graduate school career, I dated extensively. I went to a lot of dances where one could meet singles. Periodically, I would meet someone I thought was special. One relationship was serious enough that I invited the girl home for dinner. It was the first time I ever had done that. These relationships rarely lasted more than a few months. Sometimes it was the girl who ended the relationship. Usually it was I. I was easily infatuated, and just as easily fell out of infatuation. I was really concerned that I was too immature to have a lasting relationship that would eventuate in marriage.

In March 1958, one of my best friends, Ed Crabtree, invited me to a concert at his church. The concert was to be given by a Baptist college choir. I do not recall the reason, but I almost did not go; but at the last minute, I decided to attend—one of my better decisions! My friend also had invited the youth group from his married sister's church in Clifton, New Jersey, to the concert. He had an ulterior motive; there was a pretty blonde in the group in whom he was interested.

As is true in many churches, when a youth choir is giving a concert, it is customary for families in the congregation to take a few students home to house them overnight. Ed's family had extended such an invitation. They also planned a party for after the concert with the students, the youth group, and a stray (me) in attendance. During the concert, I glanced back at the youth group. There were two very pretty girls in the group. There was the blonde that Ed was pursuing, so she was "out of bounds." There also was a beautiful brunette, but she looked too young for me. I thought she was around seventeen years old. Well, the choir concert was great, but the rest of the evening did not look promising!

After the concert, while Ed took the youth group on a tour of his church, I tagged along. The tour ended in the lobby of the church. Ed then began to give the drivers instructions to his house. At the end of the instructions, he said, "Let's see, Paul, you came by yourself. Would anyone like to drive over with Paul?" After what seemed like an eternity of silence, this voice piped up and said, "Well, I can go with him." It was June. What a compassionate soul!

At the party, we sat next to each other and got acquainted. I realized that she was a bit older than seventeen. I later found out she was just shy of twenty-one. (Hooray!) At the end of the party, I asked her for her phone number. I was unaware that this presented her with a dilemma. June had a prior interest in Ed. Ed was interested in the blonde, and she was interested in the youth director. Talk about love triangles. We had a rectangle! June made a wise decision. (I am showing a slight bias here.) She gave me her number, and we started to date. This time, I did not fall out of infatuation. Fortunately, neither did she. We fell in love, and eighteen months to the date, we were married during my last year of graduate school. Our love has grown over the years, and I honestly feel that I love her more than ever. We recently celebrated our forty-ninth wedding anniversary. And, oh by the way, she still looks younger than her age!

From time to time, I have wondered what would have happened if I had followed my original inclination not to go to the concert. What would have happened if June did not pipe up to drive over with me? The chances are we would not have sat together at the party. However, I believe the Lord intended us to be together, at the party and thereafter. If I had made the decision not to go to the concert, I like to think that he would have presented other options to bring us together. Fortunately for me, it was not necessary; I had decided to go. Perhaps the Holy Spirit guided my thoughts into a wise decision. I like to think so. The situation fits one of my favorite Bible verses: "And we know that in all things God works for the good of those who love him, who have been called according to his purpose" (Romans 8:28).

YOU CAN'T OUT-GIVE GOD!

We spent our first year of marriage in married students' housing at Rutgers University. Our apartment was in an old World War II barracks section, which was quite run down. After receiving my Ph.D., I went to work at what was then known as Bell Telephone Laboratories (BTL), at Murray Hill, New Jersey, the premier research facility in the world at that time, and a part of AT&T. We rented an apartment in a large former single-family house. The owner was a widow whose late husband, a carpenter, had built the house. We occupied the upper floor of this wonderful lady's home. Our goal was to save enough money for a down payment on our own home.

We had been going to church regularly, and we made contributions, but had not been tithing (giving at least one-tenth of our income to the work of the Lord, as proscribed in the Bible). One weekend, convicted that we should be tithing, we discussed it and prayed about it. We decided we would begin tithing right away.

When I went back to work on the following Monday, I received a very interesting bit of information from a friend who shared a laboratory with me. He was a Ph.D. from the University of Iowa. He told me about a lawsuit brought against the IRS by a graduate student from another state. The graduate student had been working on a research assistantship. That meant that he was paid for doing research and development work for the university. If fortunate enough to obtain an assistantship, students work for their subsistence while involved in graduate school studies. The income from assistantships had been taxable income for many years. The aforementioned student won his case, which declared income from assistantships nontaxable, thereby setting a precedent.

My friend and I had the same situations during our graduate school careers. We were both on paid assistantships while doing our Ph.D. programs, and had paid taxes on the income. We both filled out the appropriate paperwork, and we obtained documentation from our respective universities. I was successful in my application, receiving a large refund. Unfortunately, the IRS office in Iowa denied my friend's application.

As I recall, the amount we received was just enough to give us the down payment on the house we desired. I know that one could be cynical about the idea that God rewarded us for our decision to tithe. He does not always reward financial giving with direct remuneration, as I believe was the situation in our case. However, I believe that God blesses faithfulness, not necessarily financially, but in many ways in life, as he chooses. In our case, I believe he was teaching us a lesson that was appropriate for us at that time.

LIFE IS WHAT HAPPENS TO YOU WHILE YOU ARE PLANNING SOMETHING ELSE

During the last months of my Ph.D. program at Rutgers University, I began to interview at various companies, looking for the right environment for my research interests. As mentioned previously, Bell Telephone Laboratories (BTL) hired me. A friend of mine was very helpful during my application process at Bell. He had been a graduate student at Rutgers while I was an undergrad in the same department of the College of Engineering. I sent him my resume and he saw to it that it went to the appropriate person in the Human Resources Department.

After about six months in a semiconductor program, a reorganization eliminated the program although it had been progressing very well. It was fortuitous that I was assigned to a project on a memory device for computers. My friend who had helped with my application had invented the device. He also had been rewarded for his performance with a promotion to department manager at Allentown, PA. His department in Allentown was a development facility that supported the Western Electric manufacturing group destined to produce the magnetic memory device he invented.

At Murray Hill, I was transferred to a group headed by a brilliant physicist, Dr. Michael Gyorgy. Our task was to continue with refinements in the memory device. After this program ended, we continued to work in the area of materials for computer devices. Mike was great at developing theories of behavior in such materials. Supported by a laboratory with skilled materials fabricators and technicians, I did the practical work of developing materials that proved the theories. It was an exciting time. I loved my work. I presented technical papers at professional society gatherings, and published papers in technical journals. We were known worldwide for our work. We received a number of patents. At the time, I planned to stay at BTL throughout my career. Suddenly, everything changed.

Our department management team was reorganized. We had a terrific department manager, Hutch Looney, who was promoted to Laboratory Director in another part of the company. The man who took his place had occasional disagreements with Mike, so our management thought it best to transfer Mike to another department. Unfortunately, they would not let his team go with him. I was assigned to a very good friend who had done creative device work, but as he would agree, his expertise was not in materials. I no longer had a supervisor who would be able to team up with me on R & D work. Our new department manager, with whom I got along well, told me the company was going to set up a new materials laboratory, and I would be assigned to that function.

As time went by, I became more dissatisfied with my isolated circumstance. Over the months, I had been praying for God to improve my situation. I decided to call my friend in Allentown where they were doing work in my area, knowing they could use my help. I visited him to see what possibility there would be for a transfer. I thought that he would be delighted to have me in his group. I was surprised at his lack of encouragement. I inquired if there would be a level of support for my work as I had at Murray Hill—assistants and technical workers. He did not promise such support. The door seemed to be shut tightly on this direction.

I went home greatly discouraged, and after many more months went by, I began to work on my resume. One evening, the phone rang, and it was a man named Dr. Irving Wolf. The pioneer company in tape recording, Ampex Corporation in Redwood City, California was starting a magnetic materials group, and someone familiar with my work recommended me to head up the group. I was never able to find out who this benefactor was.

I went out to Redwood City for the interview, but was greatly disappointed. Although the research and development challenge was right up my alley, there were some drawbacks. There was not much equipment—I had more in my personal laboratory at BTL. Moreover, the salary offer was somewhat greater than my BTL salary, but I questioned whether it was sufficient to pull up stakes and migrate across country. On the flight home, I prayed for God's direction. As I continued to pray over the weekend, I asked God to indicate somehow what my decision should be. On Monday morning, I received a call from Dr. Bill Gross, the Vice President of the Research and Advanced Technology Division. He had been out of town at the time of my interview. He told me I had impressed the interviewers, and he felt that the salary offer was a little low. So, he added a number of stock options to the offer. I felt this was an indication from God, an answer to my prayer. I accepted the position.

When I submitted my resignation to BTL, I received an immediate phone call from my friend from Allentown. He wanted to talk to me. I visited with him for a whole day while he tried to convince me to join his department. He told me he was interested in getting me all along. He could not tell me at the time, because I had not told my management in Murray Hill first. I had not observed the proper protocol. I did not think to ask him why he did not tell me that at the time of my earlier visit. He stated that he had been trying to get me transferred to him for many months. My management did not want to release me, because they wanted me for the new materials laboratory that had not yet emerged. The door I had thought was tightly shut was in reality wide open! I told my friend that I had made a commitment, and I would not rescind it. When I returned to Murray Hill, I had a call from another Laboratory Director. I spent a whole day with him as he tried to convince me to join his laboratory. I again had to refuse because I did not want to renege on my commitment to Ampex.

We moved to California, and I worked for Ampex for 20 years. The job worked out great. My work area was very successful. We developed important materials without which Ampex would not have been able to produce the state-of-the-art tape recorders for which it was famous. We also developed a new line of microwave materials for outside sales. I started a small business within the company to manufacture the necessary materials. I received numerous promotions over the years, eventually to a general manager position. We loved the area of California in which we settled, especially the great climate. No more shoveling snow in New Jersey or Pennsylvania. We were led to a great church that we have attended for over forty years at the time of this writing. We have been extremely happy with the decision we made a long time ago.

And oh, by the way, Ampex hit a few rough years after I joined them (not my fault, honestly!), and my stock options expired "under water." I never collected a penny from the final indicator that led me to make my decision to join the company. As I stated earlier, who says that God does not have a sense of humor! Fortunately, my salary increases and later option packages far exceeded the loss of the earlier package. It would be hard to convince me that the story of how I was "crow-barred" out of BTL and led to Ampex was not the work of the Lord. A simple show of interest by my friend in Allentown could have led me in another direction that would have kept me with BTL. It is clear to me, for a lot of reasons, the Lord wanted us in California.

SO WHAT IS A COVENANT CHURCH?

Having made the decision to move, we placed our home in Bridgewater Township, New Jersey, on the market. After the sale, we set out to get ready for the trip across the USA. The moving vans arrived, and were being loaded, when the phone rang. It was one of my best friends, Dick Cossaboon. We had met Dick and his family at a local Baptist church that we were attending. We played on a basketball team together, and with our wives, frequently did a lot of fun things. Because of a job change, the Cossaboons had moved to Pennsylvania. Dick asked me, "You're going to Redwood City, aren't you?" I said that he was correct. He then said I would not believe this, but in the current issue of his alumni newspaper, there was an article on Dick Rabine, the Christian Education Director at Peninsula Covenant Church in Redwood City. The fact that made this so unusual was that these former college roommates had totally lost contact with each other. Neither knew where the other one was. Yet in that particular issue, at the time we were getting ready to go to Redwood City, there was an article on Rabine. Dick Cossaboon said, "I don't know what kind of church a Covenant church is, but if Rabine is C.E. Director, it must be a good church."

We did not know what a Covenant church was either. We found out later that there were only three Covenant churches in New Jersey, none of them near our home. Peninsula Covenant Church is part of the Evangelical Covenant Church of America denomination and has its roots in the Swedish Lutheran Church. There are many Covenant churches in the mid-West and on the West Coast.

Dick Cossaboon wrote a letter to Dick Rabine, informing him that we were moving to his area. We took a couple of weeks to go across country, visiting relatives and sightseeing. When we arrived, we contacted Rabine. He showed us the church campus (literally a campus occupying seven acres), and introduced us to some of the members of the congregation. We began attending the church and knew we had been directed to our church home. The services were similar to other "mainline" Christian churches, the music was excellent, and the preaching by Rev. Dwight Small was first rate. He later became a professor at Westmont College in Santa Barbara. We have been attending and serving at Peninsula Covenant Church for over forty-four years.

TRAGEDY AVERTED

June and I were typical of many Jerseyans in our love of what was called in New Jersey, "the shore." On the west coast, they refer to "going to the beach" or "going to the ocean." Throughout our lives, we spent a great deal of time with friends or family during the summers at the shore. The water at the shore in New Jersey gets into the high 60-degree to low 70-degree temperature range during the summers because of the Gulf Stream. Such water temperatures, while not exactly a warm bath, were fine for swimming, body surfing, water-skiing, etc.—wet suit not required!

When we were considering the Redwood City job, we checked out the location on the map and were delighted to see that the ocean was very close to where we would be located. However, we were very disappointed when we later learned that the water is frigid all year-round in Northern California. We still could enjoy picnicking or walking on the beach, but our occasional efforts at swimming were very brief. As a result, we sometimes vacationed in Southern California, where the water is much warmer. On one such vacation, we were staying at a very nice motel in La Jolla, just north of San Diego, and were having a wonderful time at the beach and in many other pleasant activities in the area. Our daughters, Lori, who was six years old, and Lisa, who was two years old, really had a great time.

One morning, June and I were in the bathroom getting ready for the day's activities. The girls were already dressed and were playing outside the motel room. As I was shaving, I suddenly experienced a premonition that something was wrong with Lisa. I put my shaver down and asked June where Lisa was. She told me Lisa was playing with Lori. So I went back to shaving. I again had the strong premonition. This time, I went outside and saw Lori alone. I asked her where Lisa was, and she told me that she did not know. In a panic, I began running down the center of the U-shaped motel. It was a very long way. Across the way on the right, I saw a maid. I called out to her to see if she had seen a little girl. She apparently did not understand English, so I yelled out again, holding my hand out about waist high. She understood and pointed farther down the "U." I ran all the way down there, and there was Lisa, sitting at the edge of the pool with her feet in the water. There was no one else in the area. Greatly relieved, I happily scooped her up and walked back to our room.

Whenever I hear of some young child drowning in the family pool or in a neighbor's pool, I frequently remember this incident. So often, it is only a very short time that the child has been left alone. It takes so little time for a child to slip into the water and be lost. So, what happened in our case? Where did the premonitions come from? I am sure the reader knows what my conclusion has been all these years. I believe that God had plans for Lisa, as well as for Lori. Both of them and their husbands have been excellent servants for the Lord. Both daughters have used their talents in music, writing, teaching, and bringing up their children (eight collectively) according to Christian principles.

As I previously mentioned, I believe the above experiences—and many more that I have not included here—are illustrative of the Holy Spirit at work. Moreover, in the spirit of fairness, I wish to express another point so the reader does not get the wrong idea. Our lives are not a continuum of situations and events clearly directed by the Lord. The selected examples have occurred over decades of time. I do believe that God has purposes for all who will submit to him. However, there are long periods where his activities are not apparent. During those decades, there were times of hardships and periods in which we wondered what God was doing, or not doing. There were periods that were tests of our faith, and we really needed to be in extensive prayer. Looking back, these were periods that invariably brought us closer to the Lord and resulted in significant spiritual growth and trust.

Although I am repeating my comment from above, I want to emphasize my trust in Romans 8:28: "And we know that in all things God works for the good of those who love him, who have been called according to his purpose." I believe that even experiences that may appear to us to be negative are occurring within the concept of the above verse. God is working out his purposes for us, our community, and all of his creation. There are always things we do not understand or cannot explain, but God is sovereign. He sees the big picture, from beginning to end. We do not. Some day, we will be with him as part of his resurrected earth, and it all will have been worth every struggle.

11

Conclusion

I write these things to you who believe in the name of the Son of God
so that you may know that you have eternal life.

1 John 5:13

THERE IT IS—IN THE verse above—the essence of what this book is all
about. The purpose is so that you may know that you have eternal
life. Those are not my words. Those are not the words of brilliant philosophers. They are the words of God according to the apostle John, and the
Lord is loving enough to have left us with a lot of evidence. At this point,
I hope that every reader understands the importance of this verse. What
could be more important than having your eternal life settled for all time
so that you can be in the presence of the loving God forever? What could
be more important than having a loving relationship with your creator
here on earth for the remainder of your lifetime—as a member of his
kingdom—drawing on his strength for a victorious life?

We have covered many weighty factors in a short number of pages.
I could have written a book on any one of the chapters. In fact many others have done so, and I have listed some of them under "Recommended
Reading." I would encourage you to dig deeper via these recommendations. My goal was to present evidence for the existence of a Creator; the
fact that he left us a most unique book, the Bible; and that he provided
us a way to have an eternal relationship with him. He is a Holy God, and
cannot coexist with sin. Each one of us needs a way to have our sins paid
for so that we can spend all eternity with him after we pass out of this
world. He provided the way through the willingness of Jesus to take upon
himself our sins.

FAITH AND EVIDENCE

The title of this book tells us that it is about evidence. I emphasize that the book is not a proof, as that negates the importance of faith. Faith is still the foundation of the relationship with our Maker. Righteous living by faith is not a crutch that preachers use to get people to trust in God. It is the Bible that teaches us "the righteous shall live by faith." This is not an isolated principle. In the very first book of the Bible, it states, "Abram believed in the Lord, and he credited to him as righteousness" (Genesis 15:6). In other words, Abram (later to be renamed Abraham) had faith in the Lord, and the Lord viewed him as righteous. Also in the Old Testament, in Habakkuk 2:4, we read, "but the righteous will live by his faith." The apostle Paul refers to these words in his book of Romans in the New Testament: "For in the Gospel a righteousness from God is revealed, a righteousness that is by faith from first to last, just as it is written: 'The righteous will live by faith'" (Romans 1:17). So, our relationship with our creator is based on our faith in God and in his Son as our Savior.

However, is it a "blind faith?" We sometimes hear that faith in God or his Son, Jesus, is a blind faith. The purpose of this book has been to refute this concept. We have seen throughout this book that there is much evidence that supports faith. Therefore, it is not blind faith at the heart of the Christian's belief system, but a logical, intelligent, reasoned faith, supported by evidence in the Scriptures and in many external sources. I believe that this is God's way of rewarding faith, by providing lots of evidence to encourage those who have committed to him and are earnestly seeking the truth.

SUMMARY

In the Introduction, I showed how a buildup of circumstantial evidence will prevail in secular court cases, suggesting also that considerable evidence for a creator, the Bible, and the Gospel exists. As many persons who believe in an evolution without a creator conclude that there is no creator, it was important to confront the flaws in such a theory. Unfortunately, such an evolutionary process is taught as a fact throughout the educational system. I showed from the work of many other authors that undirected evolution is not a fact; rather, it is a flawed, unlikely theory. Even the world's foremost atheist became a deist because of the evidence for a creator.

Ergo, the evidence strongly supports the work of an intelligent designer. I then presented evidence for the Bible's uniqueness as a "manual" from God. I showed that it was very different from the documents of other religions, as a single person wrote most other such documents; while over forty authors, in three languages, on three continents, wrote the Bible over approximately a fifteen hundred year period. I then explored various concepts that gave support to the Bible as the word of God. Among them were fulfilled prophecy, types of Christ, how God's ways are different from man's ways, and the consistency between the Old and New Testaments.

At this point, considering that many would trust the Bible is truly from God, I explained what the Bible taught as the way to attain eternal life with God, the Gospel. I presented many verses from the New Testament authors confirming that the way of salvation begins with the admission that everyone is a sinner needing the grace of God. That grace was provided by the sacrifice on the cross by Jesus Christ, taking upon himself the sins of all who would accept him as their Lord. Many of the verses that I quoted were from Jesus himself.

As additional evidence for the validity of the Gospel, I gave illustrations of lives that were transformed by accepting Jesus as Savior. I was very selective, as I could have filled volumes about so many persons whose lives were transformed. I first discussed the lives of the eleven apostles, followed by an exposition of the life of the later apostle Paul. For a more modern approach, I gave illustrations of three currently living Christian leaders who were very unlikely candidates before their commitments to Jesus Christ. I concluded the main body of the book with a number of my experiences in life that to me could only be explained by the workings of the Holy Spirit. Again, I was very selective, picking just a few stories as illustrations. I continue to have such experiences from time to time and could have included many other occurrences.

SUGGESTIONS FOR THE READER

In the Preface, I talked about target audiences who represent a number of different backgrounds—New Christians who have not had the time to grow in their knowledge of their new belief system; mature Christians who may not have developed depth of understanding over the years; students and their parents; and finally, "seekers"—persons who have not settled on a particular faith, and are still exploring various possibilities for their beliefs. For new Christians and mature Christians who have not gone into these matters in depth, the material in this book and the recommended reading should provide information that hopefully will lead to spiritual growth. For students and their parents, who will probably encounter teachers, instructors, and professors who will teach that an undirected evolution is a fact, this book can be a great help. Such instruction has destroyed the faith of many young persons who have not had the factual information presented in the first chapter. Lee Strobel, whose books are recommended in chapter one, is just such a person.[1] An attorney and journalist, he gave up religious belief until he did a serious exploration of the truth as a mature adult. He now is a Christian and a prolific writer of books that support Christian beliefs. One literary agent who read my chapter on the problems with evolution stated that he wished he had my book as a freshman in college. For such persons, this book can be a great way to prepare for the onslaught from ignorant or destructive proponents of Godless evolution.

Finally, I wish to address "seekers"—those who are genuinely trying to find the truth—those who have a hunger for a relationship with their Creator. In my opinion, this section of the book may be the most important. Seekers are very important to God. In the words of Jesus: "In the same way, I tell you, there is rejoicing in the presence of angels of God over one sinner who repents" (Luke 15:10). If you are a seeker, I hope that this book has provided the answers that will help you to make a decision to accept Jesus as Lord. If it has not, I hope that it will lead you to attend an Evangelical Protestant or Evangelical Roman Catholic church to continue your search; or find a solid Christian friend to have a dialog on these issues. Please do not give up; it is too important.

For seekers who have seen in chapter seven the way to have their sins forgiven and desire to become followers of Jesus Christ, what should they do next? Here is my heartfelt hope for you and my recommendation to you: In your own words, pray to the Lord confessing that you know you have sinned, as we all have according to the Bible, and you want to be forgiven. Tell the Lord that you believe in Jesus Christ as Savior and you accept his sacrifice on the cross as payment for your sins. As an example, here is a typical prayer of this type:[2]

1. Lee Strobel, *The Case for Christ*. Grand Rapids: Zondervan, 1998, 13.

2. Rev. Gary Gaddini, Redwood City, CA, Peninsula Covenant Church, private communication.

> Father God, I believe Jesus is the door to me becoming who I was created to be. He proved it by rising from the dead. Please forgive me for all my sins. Thank you, Jesus, for dying and rising from the dead for me. Today, I am walking through the door and choose to follow you as my Lord and Savior. Fill me and guide me with your Holy Spirit. Thank you for your free gift of eternal life. Amen.

I have three more recommendations. First, find an Evangelical Protestant or Evangelical Roman Catholic church to attend so that you may grow in your new faith. Secondly, find a few other Christians, hopefully your friends, and tell them about your decision. They will want to encourage you and pray for you. They will also be good resources for you if you have questions about spiritual matters. Most importantly, do not delay in making your decision for Christ. As support for my suggestion, I will relate two stories about close friends who had opportunities to make the same decision. The first one was a very close friend in college decades ago. He attended a church where they taught moral principles and that it was desirable to be a good person. They did not teach the truth of the Gospel. I explained to him about the teachings that one needed to accept Jesus as Savior for one's sins. He did not disagree, but he said that he might make such a decision in the future. He did not feel ready to make the decision at that time. A few years ago he had a major heart attack and came very close to losing his life. To my knowledge, he has still not made the decision.

The second one was a business associate who became a very good friend. Even after we both left the company where we worked, we and our wives continued to get together for dinners at one home or the other, or at restaurants. He and his wife later left the Bay Area, but we maintained contact by phone. We had many opportunities to discuss faith, as he was not yet a believer. Unfortunately, he developed a terminal health condition that lingered for many months. He came to know the Gospel very well, but as he expressed it, he just could not make the decision. In our phone conversations, he never said how close he was to the end. Then I received a phone call from his wife—he had passed away. My hope is that during the last hours of his life he did pray for forgiveness. One might ask, "Would God honor such a last minute prayer?" Yes, he would. As evidence, I would like to relate one of my favorite parables of Jesus found in Matthew 20:1–15:

> For the kingdom of heaven is like a landowner who went out early in the morning to hire men to work in his vineyard. He agreed to

pay them a denarius for the day and sent them into his vineyard. About the third hour he went out and saw others standing in the marketplace doing nothing. He told them, "You also go and work in my vineyard, and I will pay you whatever is right." So they went. He went out again about the sixth hour and the ninth hour and did the same thing. About the eleventh hour he went out and found still others standing around. He asked them, "Why have you been standing here all day long doing nothing?" "Because no one has hired us," they answered. He said to them, "You also go and work in my vineyard." When evening came, the owner of the vineyard said to his foreman, "Call the workers and pay them their wages, beginning with the last ones hired and going on to the first." The workers who were hired about the eleventh hour came and each received a denarius. So when those came who were hired first, they expected to receive more. But each one of them also received a denarius. When they received it, they began to grumble against the landowner. "These men who were hired last worked only one hour," they said, "and you have made them equal to us who have borne the burden of the work and the heat of the day." But he answered one of them, "Friend, I am not being unfair to you. Didn't you agree to work for a denarius? Take your pay and go. I want to give the man who was hired last the same as I gave you. Don't I have the right to do what I want with my own money? Or are you envious because I am generous?"

Upon a quick reading, we might feel sympathetic for the earlier workers. Why should all get the same wage? However, there is more here than a simplistic reading. Remember that it is Jesus telling this parable, so it has deep meaning. He says that it is about the kingdom of heaven. First, a denarius, even for a whole day's labor, was a very generous wage. Secondly, it is important to understand this parable is a metaphor for God's saving grace. The landowner is symbolic of God. The workers are representative of people coming to him in repentance and accepting God's gift of eternal life. It does not matter at what stage of life one accepts Jesus as Savior. A common error made by those turning down God's gift is that they have led long lives of sin, and it is too late to come to the Lord in repentance. It is never too late!

However, I would also like to present another parable for people like my friend who made an unwise decision about the direction for his life. Again this is a lesson from Jesus.

And he told them this parable: "The ground of a certain rich man produced a good crop. He thought to himself, 'What shall I do? I have no place to store my crops.' Then he said, 'This is what I'll do. I will tear down my barns and build bigger ones, and there I will store all my grain and my goods. And I'll say to myself, you have plenty of good things laid up for many years. Take life easy; eat, drink and be merry.' But God said to him, 'You fool! This very night your life will be demanded from you. Then who will get what you have prepared for yourself?'" (Luke 12:16–20).

Again the parable is not really about riches. It is about making secular decisions for one's selfish desires versus making spiritual decisions to be committing oneself to God's direction for eternal life. One never knows when their life will be "demanded" from them. One of my best friends died of a major heart attack at the age of forty-seven years old. Fortunately, he had long before accepted Jesus as his Savior. I look forward to seeing him some day when my days are ended.

Please do not delay. Your life is important to God. Make that decision now. You will never regret it, and you will be surprised by the wonderful changes in your life.

Appendix A

I N ADDITION TO THE verses that I cited in chapter seven, I include here many other statements by Jesus that support the concept of the Gospel. I recommend that the reader look up these verses in his/her Bible as additional edification. It is also recommended that the verses before and after those below be read to understand the context.

WHAT DID JESUS SAY?

Matthew 4:17: "Repent, for the kingdom of heaven is near."

Matthew 4:19: "Come, follow me."

Matthew 9:2–7: "Some men brought to him a paralytic, lying on a mat. When Jesus saw their faith, he said to the paralytic, 'Take heart, son: your sins are forgiven.' At this, some of the teachers of the law said to themselves, 'This fellow is blaspheming!' Knowing their thoughts, Jesus said, 'Why do you entertain evil thoughts in your hearts? Which is easier: to say, your sins are forgiven, or to say, Get up and walk?' But so that you may know that the Son of Man has authority on earth to forgive sins ... Then he said to the paralytic, 'Get up, take your mat and go home.' And the man got up and went home."

Matthew 9:12: "For I have not come to call the righteous, but sinners."

Matthew 9:15: "The time will come when the bridegroom will be taken from them; then they will fast."

Matthew 10:32–33: "Whoever acknowledges me before men, I will also acknowledge him before my Father in heaven. But whoever disowns me before men, I will disown him before my Father in heaven."

Matthew 11:27: "All things have been committed to me by my Father. No one knows the Son except the Father, and no one knows the Father except the Son and those to whom the Son chooses to reveal him."

Matthew 12:30: "He who is not with me is against me and he who does not gather with me scatters."

Matthew 18:3: "And he said, 'I tell you the truth, unless you change and become like little children, you will never enter the kingdom of heaven.'"

Matthew 26:28: "This is my blood of the covenant, which is poured out for many for the forgiveness of sins."

Matthew 28:18–20: "Then Jesus came to them and said, 'All authority in heaven and on earth has been given to me. Therefore go and make disciples of all nations, baptizing them in the name of the Father and of the Son and of the Holy Spirit, and teaching them to obey everything I have commanded you.'"

Mark 1:15: "The time has come," he said. "The kingdom of God is near. Repent and believe the good news!"

Mark 2:5: "When Jesus saw their faith, he said to the paralytic, 'Son, your sins are forgiven.'"

Mark 2:17: "It is not the healthy who need a doctor but the sick. I have not come to call the righteous, but sinners."

Mark 10:45: "For even the Son of Man did not come to be served, but to serve, and to give his life as a ransom for many."

Mark 16:15–16: "Go into all the world and preach the good news to all creation. Whoever believes and is baptized will be saved, but whoever does not believe will be condemned."

Mark 11:8–9: "I tell you, whoever acknowledges me before men, the Son of Man will also acknowledge him before the angels of God. But he who disowns me before men will be disowned before the angels of God."

Mark 13:3: "But unless you repent, you too will perish."

Mark 15:10: "In the same way, I tell you, there is rejoicing in the presence of the angels of God over one sinner who repents."

Luke 18:10–14: "Two men went up to the temple to pray, one a Pharisee and the other a tax collector. The Pharisee stood up and prayed about himself: 'God, I thank you that I am not like other men—robbers, evildoers, adulterers—or even like this tax collector. I fast twice a week and give a tenth of all I get.' But the tax collector stood at a distance. He would not even look up to heaven, but beat his breast and said, 'God have mercy on me, a sinner.' I tell you that this man, rather than the other, went home justified before God."

Luke 19:10: "For the Son of Man came to seek and to save what was lost."

Luke 21:33: "Heaven and earth will pass away, but my words will never pass away."

Luke 24:46–47: "This is what is written: The Christ will suffer and rise from the dead on the third day, and repentance and forgiveness of sins will be preached in his name to all nations, beginning at Jerusalem."

John 5:24: "I tell you the truth, whoever hears my word and believes him who sent me has eternal life and will not be condemned; he has crossed over from death to life."

John 6:47: "I tell you the truth, he who believes has everlasting life."

John 8:12: "I am the light of the world. Whoever follows me will never walk in darkness, but will have the light of life."

John 8:24: "I told you that you would die in your sins; if you do not believe that I am the one I claim to be, you will indeed die in your sins."

John 8:36: "So if the Son sets you free, you will be free indeed."

John 9:5: "While I am in the world, I am the light of the world."

John 10:9: "I am the gate; whoever enters through me will be saved."

John 10:11: "I am the good shepherd. The good shepherd lays down his life for the sheep."

John 12:32–33: "'But I, when I am lifted up from the earth, will draw all men to myself.' He said this to show the kind of death he was going to die."

John 12:46: "I have come into the world as a light, so that no one who believes in me should stay in darkness."

John 14:6: "I am the way and the truth and the life. No one comes to the Father except through me."

John 17:3: "Now this is eternal life: that they may know you, the only true God, and Jesus Christ whom you have sent."

Appendix B

As indicated in chapter seven, where I included a limited number of verses that pertained to the Gospel, I provide a number of additional references here for those who desire more details.

WHAT DID THE APOSTLE PAUL SAY?

Acts 13:22–23: (Quoting God) "'I have found David son of Jesse a man after my own heart; he will do everything I want him to do.' From this man's descendants God has brought to Israel the Savior Jesus, as He Promised."

Romans 4:25: "He was delivered over to death for our sins and was raised to life for our justification."

Romans 5:1–2: "Therefore, since we have been justified through faith, we have peace with God through our Lord Jesus Christ, through whom we have gained access by faith into this grace in which we now stand."

1 Corinthians 1:18: "For the message of the cross is foolishness to those who are perishing, but to us who are being saved it is the power of God."

1 Corinthians 15:3–8: "For what I received I passed on to you as of first importance: that Christ died for our sins according to the Scriptures, that he was buried, that he was raised on the third day according to the Scriptures, and that he appeared to Peter, and then to the Twelve. After that, he appeared to more than five hundred of the brothers at the same time, most of whom are still living, though some have fallen asleep. Then he appeared to James, then to all the apostles, and last of all he appeared to me also, as to one abnormally born."

2 Corinthians 5:18–19: "All this is from God, who reconciled us to himself through Christ and gave us the ministry of reconciliation: that God was reconciling the world to himself in Christ, not counting

men's sins against them. And he has committed to us the message of reconciliation."

2 Corinthians 5:21: "God made him who had no sin to be sin for us, so that in him we might become the righteousness of God."

Galatians 1: 3–5: "Grace and peace to you from God our Father and the Lord Jesus Christ, who gave himself for our sins to rescue us from the present evil age, according to the will of our God and Father, to whom be glory for ever and ever."

Galatians 3:26–27: "You are all sons of God through faith in Christ Jesus, for all of you who were baptized into Christ have clothed yourselves with Christ."

Galatians 4:4–5: "But when the time had fully come, God sent his Son, born of a woman, born under law, to redeem those under law, that we might receive the full rights of sons."

Ephesians 1:7–8: "In him we have redemption through his blood, the forgiveness of sins, in accordance with the riches of God's grace that he lavished on us with all wisdom and understanding."

Ephesians 2:4–5: "But because of his great love for us, God, who is rich in mercy, made us alive with Christ even when we were dead in transgressions—it is by grace you have been saved."

Ephesians 2:13: "But now in Christ Jesus you who once were far away have been brought near through the blood of Christ."

Colossians 1:13–14: "For he has rescued us from the dominion of darkness and brought us into the kingdom of the Son he loves, in whom we have redemption, the forgiveness of sins."

Colossians 2:13-14: "When you were dead in your sins and in the uncircumcision of your sinful nature, God made you alive with Christ. He forgave us all our sins, having canceled the written code, with its regulations, that was against and that stood opposed to us; he took it away, nailing it to the cross."

1 Timothy 1:15–16: "Here is a trustworthy saying that deserves full acceptance: Christ Jesus came into the world to save sinners—of whom I am the worst. But for that very reason I was shown mercy so that in me, the worst of sinners, Christ Jesus might display his unlimited patience as an example for those who would believe on him and receive eternal life."

Titus 3:4-7: "But when the kindness and love of God our Savior appeared, he saved us, not because of righteous things we had done, but because of his mercy. He saved us through the washing of rebirth and renewal by the Holy Spirit, whom he poured out on us generously through Jesus Christ our Savior, so that, having been justified by his grace, we might become heirs having the hope of eternal life."

Hebrews 8:26–27: "Such a high priest meets our need—one who is holy, blameless, pure, set apart from sinners, exalted above the heavens. Unlike the other high priests, he does not need to offer sacrifices day after day, first for his own sins, and then for the sins of the people. He sacrificed for their sins once for all when he offered himself."

WHAT DID THE APOSTLE PETER SAY?

Acts 2:21: "And everyone who calls on the name of the Lord will be saved."

Acts 3:18–19: "But this is how God fulfilled what he had foretold through all the prophets, saying that his Christ would suffer. Repent, then, and turn to God, so that your sins may be wiped out, that times of refreshing may come from the Lord."

Acts 5:31: "God exalted him to his own right hand as Prince and Savior that he might give repentance and forgiveness of sins to Israel."

1 Peter 1:18–20: "For you know that it was not with perishable things such as silver or gold that you were redeemed from the empty way of life handed down to you from your forefathers, but with the precious blood of Christ, a lamb without blemish or defect. He was chosen before the creation of the world, but was revealed in these last times for your sake."

2 Peter 3:9: "The lord is not slow in keeping his promise, as some understand slowness. He is patient with you, not wanting anyone to perish, but everyone to come to repentance."

WHAT DID THE APOSTLE JOHN SAY?

John 20:30–31: "Jesus did many other miraculous signs in the presence of his disciples, which are not recorded in this book. But these are written that you may believe that Jesus is the Christ, the Son of God, and that by believing you may have life in his name."

1 John 1:7–10: "But if we walk in the light, as he is in the light, we have fellowship with one another, and the blood of Jesus, his Son, purifies us from all sin. If we claim to be without sin, we deceive ourselves and the truth is not in us. If we confess our sins, he is faithful and just and will forgive us our sins and purify us from all unrighteousness. If we claim we have not sinned, we make him out to be a liar and his word has no place in our lives."

1 John 2:23: "No one who denies the Son has the Father; whoever aknowledges the Son has the Father also."

1 John 3:5: "But you know that he appeared so that he might take away our sins."

1 John 4:14–15: "And we have seen and testify that the Father has sent his Son to be the Savior of the world. If anyone acknowledges that Jesus is the Son of God, God lives in him and he in God."

1 John 5:5: "Who is it that overcomes the world? Only he who believes that Jesus is the Son of God."

WHAT DID THE APOSTLE MARK SAY?

Mark 1:4–5: "And so John came, baptizing in the desert region and preaching a baptism of repentance for the forgiveness of sins. The whole Judean countryside and all the people of Jerusalem went out to him. Confessing their sins, they were baptized by him in the Jordan River."

WHAT DID JOHN THE BAPTIST SAY?

John 1:35–36: "The next day John was there again with two of his disciples. When he saw Jesus passing by, he said, 'Look, the Lamb of God!'"

Appendix C

Family History and the Gospel

*I will pour out my Spirit on your offspring,
and my blessing on your descendants.*

Isaiah 44:3

IN THE MAIN BODY of the text, I state that I am a Christian and have been for many years. The story of how I became a Christian is important to the main precepts of the book. After all, the subtitle is *A Scientist Believes in the Gospel of Jesus Christ*. However, the thread of belief that starts as far back as my maternal great-grandmother is too long to include in the main text. I place it here in this appendix so that the reader can see how God had his hand on my family, consistent with the Bible verse from Isaiah, quoted above.

I will now flash back to many decades before I was born, to a story of which I was only partially aware until I read the autobiography of my maternal grandfather, Kasha (Reverend) Mooshi Dooman, translated by my uncle, Gershom Dooman, who also added later information.[1] This document was not available until 1956, when I was twenty-three years old. The reason for this flashback is to show how God was involved in my family many generations before I was even born.

GRANDFATHER'S STORY

I knew that my maternal grandfather was a minister in what was then called Persia, now known as Iran. As a youth, I did not know much about

---

1. Rev. Mooshi Dooman, with Gershom Dooman, unpublished autobiography.

his background, other than what my mother told me. As she was orphaned at twelve years old, there was a large gap in the family history. Assyrians, whose homeland had been lost centuries before, had communities in Turkey, Iraq, and Iran. In Iran, the main location was in the northern section, near Turkey, and centered in the area of a large body of water, Lake Urmia. Our family was part of the Persian Assyrian community. The Assyrians, who belonged to several Christian denominations, were surrounded by Muslims for centuries, a very dangerous condition. Several theories have been proposed as to how the Assyrians became Christians amidst the masses of Islam. Most have proposed that the apostle Thomas evangelized them (See reference in chapter eight). Much later, there were missionary outposts present in the area.

Grandfather originally was planning to become a doctor. However, his mother wanted him to go into the ministry. Her prayers eventually won out and he became a Presbyterian minister and the first missionary ever to the Persian Muslims, starting a church in the Kurdish community in Kermanshah. His vocation meant that his life was in constant danger. He was very bold in encountering Muslims and Jews, who were also numerous in the area. While the Jews were cordial and eager to engage in discourse, the reverse was true of most Muslims. As stated in my uncle's segment of the writing, my grandfather preached to "the most fanatical people of the world at that time." Grandfather's life was in constant danger. On more than one occasion, he was beaten badly and was stoned. One Muslim, who had killed before, had threatened that he would kill Grandfather. Another man actually drew a sword and was about to kill him when a Mullah stopped the man. Muslims beheaded his first convert, and the convert's body was dragged through the streets.

A major turning point took place in the destiny of the Persian Assyrians during World War I. The Assyrians fought on the side of the Allies, and they received considerable support from the Russian Army. After years of battling against the numerically superior Turks and Kurds, the Assyrians had run out of ammunition. Moreover, the Russians had to withdraw because of the Russian Revolution. In the South of Iran, the British were in contact with the Assyrians, encouraging them to fight their way south, and the British would meet them. Out of ammunition and other supplies, the Assyrians began a massive retreat to the south. When they arrived at the rendezvous location, the British were nowhere to be found.

Many lost their lives on the way. My grandmother became ill and died of dysentery. My Uncle Gershom carried her body, while my twelve-year-old mother carried his rifle. The night that they arrived in Hamadan in central Iran, my grandfather passed away, also of dysentery. He was forty-five years old. Many years later, my uncle visited Kermanshah. Grandfather was still revered by large numbers of persons in that community, especially his converts, but also many Muslims and Jews whom he had engaged in spiritual discussions. I believe that blessings that have been experienced by my family are because of this saintly man, as indicated in the Bible verse at the head of this chapter.

MOM'S AND DAD'S STORY

My mother was placed in a Presbyterian orphanage in Hamadan, and as a young adult, she attended a Presbyterian nursing school. My father, who did not know my mother at that time, had earlier gone to Russia at age twelve to work as a painter. He eventually came to the United States and like many immigrants, started a small store in Elizabeth, New Jersey, selling produce and canned goods. His mother, in Iran, arranged the marriage to my mother. They were married in Canada, where my father had relatives. They then settled in Elizabeth. Because of my mother's history in the Presbyterian denomination, it was natural to attend a church of that denomination which was located about a mile from our home.

MY STORY

I was born in the "Port" section of Elizabeth, New Jersey, on December 15, 1932 during the Depression years. I attended Sunday School regularly all during my elementary school years. I was taught belief in God, Bible stories, and about moral behavior. Salvation as a result of accepting Jesus Christ's sacrifice was not taught at this church. Meanwhile there were other spiritual activities that influenced my life. In my neighborhood, one of my young playmates was a Christian. I was around nine or ten years old at the time. Once a week, they invited youngsters into their home for refreshments and Bible stories told by a young lady from their church. Our church suspended Sunday School during the summer months. So, invited to my neighbor's church, I attended their church's Daily Vacation Bible School and their Sunday School during that summer. I really loved the church and the basics of the Gospel that were taught. When summer was over and our Sunday

School resumed, I wanted to continue at the neighbor's church. My mother would not allow it, so I returned to our church.

During World War II, my mother had worked very hard in factories manufacturing military clothing. There were great stress and health issues in her life. She found peace by receiving Jesus Christ as her Savior. She tried to explain the basics of the Gospel to her friends at our church, including the pastor and other church officials, all of whom were very close friends. Her efforts at enlightening them were rejected.

An elderly Assyrian man, who was also a strong Christian from another denomination, advised my mother to attend an evangelical church, where the Gospel of Jesus Christ was proclaimed. He wisely explained that as a new Christian, she needed to be in an environment of loving support, Christian education, and spiritual growth. As a result, we moved to another nearby church where the Gospel was preached and all the basics of the Bible were taught. Who says God does not have a sense of humor? Here was Mom, who resisted my attending a Gospel church's Sunday school, moving us to a Gospel-centered church.

At that point, neither my father nor I had accepted Jesus Christ as Savior. My mother constantly tried to get us to understand the word of God on this subject. We both resisted strongly. However, I gradually saw the logic of her teaching. Moreover, I was also learning a great deal in the new church. During one summer, I attended a Christian youth camp. In the first large gathering of the whole camp, the invitation was given for all who would like to accept Christ as Savior to come forward, much the same as is done at a Billy Graham rally. I immediately went forward.

It was not emotional; there were no thunderclaps or bolts of lightning. It was a simple logical decision. Although for many persons, making this decision has a significant emotional content, and that is fine, it was not the case for me. However, my life was changed forever—not perfection—at times I still did things that I was ashamed of, but there was a clear change of direction. The Bible teaches that when we accept Christ as Savior, the Holy Spirit enters our lives for spiritual growth and development. In 1 John 1:9, we read a message to Christians: "If we confess our sins, He is faithful and just and will forgive us our sins and purify us from all unrighteousness." When I commit a sin, usually unintentionally, I confess it and ask for forgiveness. The grace of God is bountiful! Even now, after so many years, I feel that I am still developing. However, as I look back over the years, I can see that I have come a long way. It is not because I am a nice guy, or my basic nature leads me to seek forgiveness. Truth be told, it is just the opposite. As my loving wife would tell you, I can be volatile at times. Thankfully, God is quick to forgive when we repent. I know that my "new and improved" direction is because of the Holy Spirit in my life, at times admonishing me, at times comforting me. That is the source of power that makes me want to please God. What I know is that I would not have followed this growth path if it were not for the work of the Holy Spirit in my life. I know that I would not be the person that I am today without such a work. To me, this growth is the evidence of a special force in my life, the Holy Spirit. I have no other way to explain it.

THE "THREAD" CONTINUES

The family thread, to which I referred above, has not ended with me, but continues for two more generations. In my generation, my brother Tom is a believer. In the next generation, both of my daughters, Lori Hagen and Lisa Lauffer are long-time Christians, as are their husbands, Brent and Karl. Both daughters and their husbands are extensively involved in their churches in Christian service activities.

Lori has been a member of the choir, serves on her church board, for many years directed the children's choirs, and taught Sunday school. She also has sung solos, played the piano, and has acted in dramas in various church services and activities. On the side, she has her own business as a Creative Memories consultant, and a former teacher, she has returned to substitute teaching. Lori's husband, Brent has his own CPA firm, and he has been the church Treasurer for many years and a member of the church board. They have six children, ranging in age from seven to eighteen at the time of this writing.

Lisa was a full-time editor for a publisher of Christian youth materials, and now she has expanded her career in her home as an editor, a writer, and a life coach. She also serves on her church's worship team in Sunday services, singing in a group and also performing solos, playing the piano, and acting in dramas. Her husband, Karl, is also very active, having served as Chairman of the Church and in other Christian activities. Karl is a rocket scientist who is responsible for software on the Mars program. Lisa and Karl have two children, aged seven and eleven at the time of this writing. All of the grandchildren have accepted Jesus Christ as their Savior and are involved in service activities.